A FALL AFTERNOON IN THE GROS VENTRE RANGE

WIND-RIPPLED SAND AT BRUNEAU DUNES STATE PARK, IDAHO

AUTUMN GROUND COVER IN THE SELWAY-BITTERROOT WILDERNESS

WINTER DUSK ON THE SALMON RIVER

THE TETONS MIRRORED IN JENNY LAKE, WYOMING

A LAVA RIDGE IN CRATERS OF THE MOON NATIONAL MONUMENT

FAREWELL BEND ON THE SNAKE RIVER JUST ABOVE HELLS CANYON

THE SNAKE RIVER COUNTRY

THE AMERICAN WILDERNESS/TIME-LIFE BOOKS/NEW YORK

BY DON MOSER
AND THE EDITORS OF TIME-LIFE BOOKS

The Author: Don Moser's love affair with the Snake River country dates back to his college days when he worked as a Forest Service fire lookout in northern Idaho, and as a seasonal ranger and naturalist in Grand Teton National Park. He later spent 12 years with LIFE as a writer, bureau chief in Los Angeles and Hong Kong, and assistant managing editor. On leave from LIFE in the early '60s, he served as special assistant to then Interior Secretary Stewart Udall. Now a freelancer, Moser specializes in writing about natural history and the out-of-doors. He is the author of *The Peninsula,* a book about Olympic National Park, and of a forthcoming novel, *Summer of the Hawk.*

The Cover: The bleak chasm of Hells Canyon confines the Snake River's flow along the Idaho-Oregon border. On a 30-mile stretch of the river in this area, the canyon walls, shown here dusted with March snow, leap as high as 8,000 feet from the riverbed.

Contents

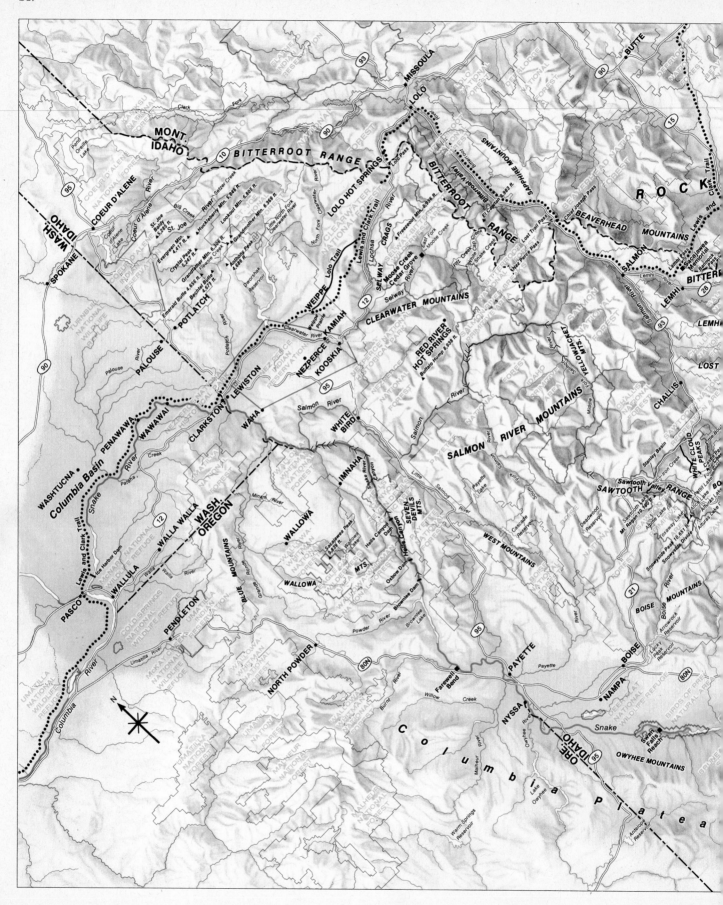

A Great River's Vast and Varied Domain

The Snake River country (green rectangle above) is detailed on the map at left, spreading over most of the state of Idaho and including slices of Montana, Wyoming, Oregon and Washington. This great stretch of U.S. wilderness contains nine million acres of mountains, deserts and forests —a remote domain where mountain ranges are twisted into mazes and where rivers run every way but east. The land is mostly within the great sickle-curve of the Snake River, which flows for a thousand miles from its Wyoming source to join the Columbia River in Washington State.

On the map at left, the blue lines are waterways, and lakes are shown in white. Federally supervised areas are outlined in red: thin red lines mark national forests; thick red lines encircle wildlife refuges, national parks, Indian reservations, forest wildernesses, and primitive and scenic areas. Double lines with numbered ovals show highways; single black lines, trails. V's on rivers indicate rapids; lines across rivers are dams; short black parallel lines are mountain passes. Black dots trace the route of the Lewis and Clark expedition; squares denote additional points of special interest.

1/ "The Accursed Mad River"

...the river was compressed into a space of less than thirty feet in width, between two ledges of rocks, upwards of two hundred feet high, and formed a whirling and tumultuous vortex. WASHINGTON IRVING/ ASTORIA

It is never really quiet on this river, though sometimes the sound is as subtle as the ocean's voice in a sea shell held to the ear. But the sound is always there: the roar of rapids. You hear it first as no more than that sea shell's voice. Then the sound comes a little louder. Then you see something—just a faint, occasional flicker of white, way down where the river disappears around a bend. The flicker appears and vanishes so quickly that you are not sure if your eyes are playing tricks. The moment is like that in the film *Lord of the Flies* when the sign of a great beast flickers above the crest of a hill so briefly that you cannot be certain what you are seeing, or even if you have seen anything at all.

A couple of hundred yards before we got to the rapids, Jim Campbell, the river guide, pulled our big rubber raft out of the water. By that time the roar had obliterated all other sound, and the faint flicker had turned into towers and gouts of water shooting up out of the river. We climbed along the rocky bank to a point where we could get a look. Campbell stared down and said over the din, "I remember the first time I ran it. Scared hell out of me." After a moment he said, "Still does."

Wild Sheep, the place is called. Here the Snake, forced into a narrow channel, races down in a long tongue, swift and smooth and looking like a piece of watered green silk. On the left side of the river is a rock the size of a house. The water goes over it as a pale, translucent billow, then comes down the back side in a white wall. Beyond the rock is a dark hole in the water, looking like the mouth of a well, big enough to swallow us, rafts and all. Farther out and below the huge rock there is a smaller rock that turns that side of the river into a white boil. Fifty yards farther downstream are three standing waves—hydraulics, boatmen sometimes call them. The waves surge straight up into the air like uphill waterfalls. These standing waves run halfway across the river, and they are 10 feet high.

"Look at that rock, boiling up down there," said Campbell.

I looked at it.

Jim Campbell is a professional riverman, and cool. We stood there for quite some time, just looking—Campbell and I and three other boatmen, along with a dozen more men, most of them Forest Service people.

"Well, I'm going to run that left tongue," Campbell said finally.

Rick Petrillo, one of the other boatmen, said, "I'll try the center."

Campbell was leading the trip, and Rick had never seen this river before, but he had run the Grand Canyon 63 times and liked to go with the big water, so Campbell just nodded.

Back at the raft we got ready. I took off my binoculars and lashed them to the raft. I took off my hat, an old friend, and tied it down too. Beside me a young forest ranger took off his shoes as if preparing for a swim. I felt that old tightening of the innards.

Campbell pushed off into the current. Petrillo's raft, ahead of us, was already sliding down the tongue toward the big rock. "I don't think he's going to make it," somebody said. "You want to wait and watch him go through, Jim?"

"I don't like to watch people go through," Campbell said.

We were picking up speed now. In the still water above us a small-mouth bass rose; a ring spread over the smooth water. I wished I was fishing. A merganser came by, fast, headed downstream, long neck out straight, wings flashing against the snow-white body. Ahead of us Petrillo's raft simply dropped out of sight, as if it had gone over a waterfall.

We were in the fast left tongue then, ripping along on the silky green water, then into the slot and sideslipping downhill, Campbell pumping back on the oars as he tried to keep us from wrapping on the big rock. He pumped, then pumped again. We kissed the edge of the rock and swept past, and I looked down into the enormous hole that seemed to run right to the bottom of the river. We whirligigged around and hit the first standing wave. It threw the raft straight up into the air; we hung there for a moment, then nose-dived into the trough, water drenching us. The second wave loomed. The raft climbed it slowly, reached the summit, slid down the other side, then up and over the third wave and we were out, roller-coasting over the smaller waves below. I looked back at Campbell. He was grinning.

The place is Hells Canyon, where a great river forms the boundary between Idaho and Oregon. The river is the Snake. And although it ranks sixth among the rivers of the United States, it is not one that most people can trace easily on their mental maps. The Snake is not a linear river like the Mississippi but a roughly semicircular one that flows for long distances in every direction but east. Visualize the river as a question mark lying on its back. The source is in the mountains near Yellowstone Park in northwestern Wyoming; the bend of the question mark sweeps in a long arc south and west across Idaho. Then it strikes north along the Idaho-Oregon line, and finally the shank angles west again through the state of Washington until it connects with the Columbia River near the city of Pasco.

The Snake is perhaps best understood in terms of the work it does —draining the western slopes of the northern Rocky Mountains into the Columbia. Thus the Snake approximates in some ways a mythical stream postulated by early explorers and cartographers—the River of the West, on which one might easily float down to the Pacific from the height of the Continental Divide. Of course the River of the West does not exist, but the Snake comes closer than anything else to fulfilling the old concept. For it is, by any measure, a mighty stream, whose waters travel more than 1,000 miles from source to mouth. But to me the unique and magnetic thing about the river today is that within the great arc of its watershed lies the largest piece of wilderness in the United States outside of Alaska—some nine million acres of mountain, desert and forest, without paved roads and with only a scattering of buildings and other signs of man.

This is a country of long vistas and prismatic light on distant mountains; of dry summer lightning and rain veils over the far ranges; of long, slow, sun-hammered swells of sagebrush, and snowmelt streams with water so cold it hurts your teeth to drink. Populous with eagles, this wild land is also the home of the elk, the cougar, the bighorn sheep and mountain goat, the coyote, the rattlesnake, the salmon. Here are many mountains, few roads, and places where you could wander for a long time without meeting another traveler.

Some features of the country have relatively familiar names: the Sawtooth Mountains, the River of No Return, the Bitterroots, Hells Canyon, the Tetons, the Craters of the Moon, the Lolo Trail. But the region as a whole has been nameless, so varied that no one has ever found an appropriate name for it. Locally, some people refer to the region as the Inland Empire—but that title is fitting only for chambers of commerce. We will call it the Snake River country.

Big country. One contiguous chunk of this wilderness, stretching from south of the Salmon River all the way north to the Lochsa River, is more than twice as large as Massachusetts. To cross it by trail from north to south would require a hike of about a month. By paved road, the shortest possible driving route around the same region is about 700 miles long. The country inside this trapezoidal roadway, by way of comparison with other great wild areas in the United States, is big enough to contain Yellowstone National Park, Yosemite, Glacier National Park and the Everglades—with plenty of room left over.

The Snake and its tributaries drain pieces of Wyoming, Utah, Nevada, Oregon and Washington. But most of the Snake River country lies in Idaho and includes the least-known parts of that little-known state. Interstate travelers who go through Idaho generally cross the irrigated desert of its southern plain, and have little idea of the enormous mountain wilderness that lies to the north.

Much of the Snake River country is owned by the federal government, and so the land gains a measure of protection, or at least regulation. Some three million acres of the Snake River watershed lie in legally designated Wilderness, protected from development by act of Congress. Another million and a half acres are in federally legislated Primitive Areas—wild lands on which no development may take place until the area has been studied for possible future classification as Wilderness. Other vast tracts are classified as Roadless Areas—still untouched lands that may or may not be developed in the future.

The geography of the Snake River country is confused and confusing. Rivers loop and meander and turn back upon themselves. Mountain ranges lie in a maze that baffles the eye and sets a man's internal compass spinning. A wonderfully mixed-up country, and wonderfully diverse. The elevation of the lower Snake River at Lewiston, Idaho, is only 741 feet; yet near the upper river, Grand Teton stands 13,766 feet above sea level. In summer, temperatures in the bottom of Hells Canyon reach 120°F.; at the foot of the Sawtooths in winter they drop to 45° below zero. Along Moose Creek in the Selway-Bitterroot Wilderness, you can walk under a cool canopy of cedar so dense the sun is invisible at high noon. Down at Craters of the Moon National Monument

Basalt boulders, tumbled from the sides of Hells Canyon, churn the waters of the Snake River into a white turmoil called Wild Sheep Rapids. When the water is at its peak here, waves tower up to 12 feet, and river-running boatmen shoot through the 250 yards of Wild Sheep in 50 seconds or less.

you can go for miles over barren black lava flows while your brain simmers in your skull. In the heat of summer you can find caves full of huge stalactites of ice, and in the dead of winter you can find hot springs that would boil you if you fell into them.

On the watershed of the Clearwater River in northern Idaho lies a region of rolling mountains, covered to their summits with forests of fir, spruce and pine—big trees. Farther south on the Selway River the land becomes steeper and wilder—a lean country of high peaks and glacier-polished granite. This is the home of the mountain goat, the bighorn sheep and herds of elk that browse on brushy mountainsides. Still farther south, in the neighborhood of the Salmon River, the country opens up into sunlit glades of ponderosa pine. Here are white-water rivers, and rarely traveled mountains that hold one of the largest populations of mountain lions in the United States.

Come south again toward the rivers of central Idaho to another change at the Sawtooths: a landscape of Matterhorn-shaped peaks, icy lakes, and meadows so lush and filled with wild flowers that you want to take off your clothes and roll on the ground. Farther south, the transformation is drastic—down from the cool of the high mountains and forests to the dormant volcanoes and bleak lava flows and a flat sagebrush desert that stretches to the horizon.

Across this varied sprawl of landscape, the connecting thread, the unifying geographical fact, is the Snake River. The first white men ever to see it were Lewis and Clark, who reached the lower river via the Clearwater in 1805. The first to investigate the Snake's upper reaches was probably that indefatigable traveler John Colter, an energetic young member of the Lewis and Clark expedition who split loose, on the way back from the Pacific Coast, to do some exploring on his own and discovered—among other things—the pocket of wonders that is now known as Yellowstone Park. At the time, nobody believed his stories of geysers and springs of bubbling mud, and people assumed that the wilderness had addled his brains.

But the first men who really explored the river and felt its power were the members of fur entrepreneur Wilson Price Hunt's expedition of 1811. Hunt's party was heading overland to the mouth of the Columbia, where it would join a second group that had gone round the Horn by ship; combined, the two parties would establish a place called Astoria, the main base for John Jacob Astor's Pacific Fur Company. The story of the expedition, told in Washington Irving's *Astoria*, is of an enterprise ill-fated from the beginning. Irving, who drew his account from interviews and expedition journals, tells that the leader, Wilson Price Hunt, was a businessman of "probity and worth" with plenty of sand in his gizzard but no experience of the wilderness. Many of his French-Canadian voyageurs were "arrant braggarts and coxcombs," either lazy, incompetent or too old and broken-down to be of much use in a bad country.

On the 26th of September, 1811, six months out of Saint Louis, the expedition was struggling down beside the Hoback River in what is now western Wyoming when the men came upon a great river whose "waters swept off through the valley in one impetuous stream" toward the Pacific. It was the Snake. Hunt's voyageurs were delighted. They thought that they would be able to build canoes and float all the way to the Columbia.

After a detour around a particularly difficult upper stretch of the Snake, Hunt's men rejoined the river, where they built and launched 15 canoes. The next day two canoes were swamped in the rapids and one of them was crushed on the rocks. Early optimism turned to anxiety. They were on bad water in an empty country. Irving called it "a vast wilderness of silent and apparently uninhabited mountains, without a savage wigwam upon its banks, or bark upon its waters."

On October 28 Hunt's party hit a particularly turbulent stretch of the river: "Its terrific appearance beggars all description—Hecate's cauldron was never half so agitated when vomiting even the most diabolical spells." Trying to get through, a canoe struck a rock and one of Hunt's most competent voyageurs was drowned. Disheartened, Hunt sent out scouts to check the river water below. On returning, one said the river was frightful but they might be able to launch their canoes again six miles down. Hunt told the men to try it with four canoes. They did and returned the next day, defeated. One of the canoes was carried away with all its lading, and the other three were stuck fast in the rocks of the rapids. By now, with the loss of so many supplies to the river, the expedition was down to five days' rations.

In order to range more widely for food, Hunt split his men into several small parties that set out separately overland across the great desert of the Snake River Plain. Two of the men wandered lost in the mountains all winter before they emerged on the Columbia, half starved and totally naked. One group of 11 tried to force Hells Canyon, and barely made it through alive. The unbroken lava cliffs that guarded the river were so sheer that the men had great difficulty getting down for water;

A mountain lioness, treed by a pack of hunting dogs, snarls defiance from her refuge high among the branches of a ponderosa pine.

sometimes there was not even wood for campfires. But they managed somehow and reached Astoria in mid-January.

Meanwhile, the Hunt party was suffering terribly. Half frozen and on the verge of starvation, the men had begun butchering their emaciated horses for nourishment. At one point Hunt's men caught sight of another detachment across the river "hovering like spectres of famine on the opposite bank." They appeared to be in even worse shape than Hunt's own men and looked so hunger-crazed and dangerous that at first no one wanted to ferry horsemeat over to them. Finally, a man braver than most transferred food in a hastily built canoe, and an extraordinary tragedy took place.

"A poor Canadian . . . named Jean Baptiste Prevost, whom famine had rendered wild and desperate," Irving writes, "ran frantically about the bank . . . crying out to Mr. Hunt to send the canoe for him, and take him from that horrible region of famine, declaring that otherwise he would never march another step, but would lie down there and die." When the canoe full of meat was sent over, Prevost tried to get aboard. The boatman told him to stay put; now there was meat on his side of the river. But Prevost said that it wasn't cooked yet, he'd starve before it was ready, and he wanted to cross to Hunt's side so he could have food immediately. He forced himself aboard, but as he neared the opposite shore and smelled meat roasting he went into a delirium, jumped up and started dancing until he tipped over the canoe. He died there, in the swift current.

Almost three months and 800 miles from where they had first joined the Snake, Hunt's main party left the river near where it turns north along the present Idaho-Oregon border and struck westward across the mountains of eastern Oregon. They thus avoided Hells Canyon, but they'd been through hell enough, and the voyageurs who survived would always remember the Snake by a name of their own—*La Maudite Rivière Enragée.* The Accursed Mad River.

Over the next two decades the Snake River country became a center of the fur trade, combed by mountain men who ranged its tributary streams for beaver. Jim Bridger, Kit Carson, Tom Fitzpatrick, Jedediah Smith and all the rest were there, the most engaging company of brigands, liars and rapscallions in our history. They scalped the Indians and were scalped in turn, fought the grizzly bears to a standstill, trapped the beaver clean out of the country, and made the nights ring with their drunken carouse.

They explored the country and gave the river the name it bears today. They did not call the river the Snake because rattlers live along its banks, although they do, nor because the riverbed meanders like a serpent, although it does, but very likely because they had a communications gap with the local Indians. The Shoshone, an amicable tribe much admired by the mountain men for the beauty of the women, lived largely on salmon caught from the river. Like all tribes they had a hand sign to designate their own nation—the sign meaning Shoshone was a wavering gesture, like the movement of a swimming fish, which probably said, in effect, "We are the salmon people." Misinterpreting the gesture, the mountain men called them the Snake Indians, and their river became the Snake River.

Throughout the 1820s and '30s, the mountain men got around the Snake region pretty thoroughly, but the exploration of the river would not be complete until an incredible century and a half later.

In 1970, a Grand Teton park ranger named Joe Shellenberger and a writer-photographer, Paul Lawrence, grew curious about inconsistencies in maps and descriptions of the source of the Snake. One map placed the source inside Yellowstone Park, another showed it farther south, on the boundary of the Teton National Forest. Local woodsmen claimed that the true source was a tributary called Fox Creek. Shellenberger and Lawrence were astonished at such confusion. They decided to go look for themselves.

In October, they strapped on their packs and headed up the Snake into the high wilderness north of the Teton Range, a territory almost never visited, except by a rare park ranger on patrol or an occasional hunting party in the fall. The trail was steep and poor, and the two men had to make difficult fords of rushing streams. After two days, the trail petered out entirely, but the men continued bushwhacking up the Snake, which had dwindled to a stream only 10 feet wide. On the third day, with a sense of high excitement, they reached a large spring from which water flowed in many rivulets for 20 feet along the canyon wall. Checking the canyon above, the men found nothing but a dry stream bed. The spring was the source of the Snake River. In the eighth decade of the 20th Century, someone had at last identified it.

Two cataclysmic geologic events far separated in time shaped the character of the Snake River country. The first of these was the uplifting, about 100 million years ago, of the complex metamorphic and granitic mass that formed the mountains of central Idaho. The second event, the great lava flows of the Snake River Plain, was much more recent —just yesterday in geologic time—and its effects still stun the eye as one follows the Snake on its long swing westward.

Imagine the scene more than three million years ago in what is now southern Idaho. An ocean of molten rock stretches to the horizon on all sides. Streams of lava issue from gaping mile-long fissures in the earth, flowing out in long, hot rivers, searing and covering everything they touch. Some of the lava streams are 100 feet thick and 100 miles long.

By the time that massive spurt of volcanic activity ceased, the lava covered a crescent some 300 miles long and 60 miles wide, the area known today as the Snake River Plain. On the west it abutted the similar and earlier lava flows of the Columbia Plateau. Altogether the molten rock covered more than 200,000 square miles of eastern Oregon, eastern Washington and southern and western Idaho, to depths that reached 5,000 feet or more.

For a time this country lay sere and lifeless as the moon; indeed, samples of basalt brought back by astronauts from lunar craters are almost indistinguishable from those found on the plain. (The astronauts trained here for a short while in preparation for their lunar visit.) Gradually, soil formed from decomposed lava built up to sufficient thickness to support some life. But the plain remained a forbidding country—it was here that Wilson Price Hunt and his men faced starvation—and except where the land has been irrigated it is a forbidding country still.

As the Snake crosses the southern boundary of the lava plain, no tributaries come in from the north, for this is a region of lost rivers. Streams that tumble down from the mountains simply disappear into the porous volcanic rock, ultimately feeding into the Snake through underground channels. One large stream, appropriately named the Big Lost River, vanishes near Arco, Idaho. Beneath the earth it mixes with other streams, and the mingled waters seep through the basalt for more than 100 miles before they reemerge at Thousand Springs on the Snake near Twin Falls, Idaho.

The Snake River Birds of Prey Natural Area south of Boise is a typical piece of the Snake River Plain. It is an austere landscape, lying under an unforgiving sun. Geographers call such country high desert or sagebrush desert; the sage dominates the eye, purple glinting away to silver when you squint against the sun, and here and there bright green clumps of greasewood. The land looks lean and lifeless, but creatures do live here; ground squirrels scoot back and forth like tiny windup toys. Along the highways you can sometimes see them nibbling at the tire-flattened bodies of their brothers; the desert forage that makes up most of their diet seems to leave them with a craving for meat. Jack rabbits live here. Rattlesnakes. Coyotes. And occasionally, off in a sky so bright you can hardly bear to look up, there is a speck, a flicker of wings, moving so fast that it hardly seems possible. This plain is a robber's roost for a company of magnificent cutthroats and aerial pirates, an extraordinary concentration of eagles, hawks and falcons that nest on the rugged cliffs and feed on the ground squirrels, marmots and jack rabbits of the plateau.

A steep, rough and hair-raising dirt road drops hundreds of feet down into the canyon of the Snake. Here the river twists slowly across the flat bottom that it has sliced through the old lava flows. On both sides rise vertical cliffs of basalt. They are layered; a single cliff face may show two or three separate lava flows, one on top of another. When the lava cooled, it frequently fractured into symmetrical polygonal columns. Sometimes a layer of this columnar structure, as much as 100 feet thick, will lie sandwiched between other flows, giving the cliff faces the look of a planned structure.

Here and there on the canyon floor are black boulders, so huge that even the Snake could not have moved them. They are the only remaining signs of a flood that occurred some 30,000 years ago. During a period of glaciation at that time, a huge lake known to geologists as Lake Bonneville lay south of the river. Bonneville's water gradually rose until it flowed northward into the Snake through a 400-foot pass near Pocatello, Idaho. At many places the Snake River Canyon was filled to the brim and water spilled out onto the surrounding plain as the lake-fed river rushed toward the Columbia and the Pacific. In its initial stages this great flood was so violent that it tore boulders from the surrounding slopes and rolled them for miles until they finally came to rest where they lie today, in the canyon area.

Volcanic activity along the Snake River Plain has continued until very recently. At Craters of the Moon National Monument, north of the river, the last eruptions occurred only a few thousand years ago. Were a new volcano or lava flow to emerge somewhere on the plain tomorrow, no geologist would be surprised.

The wilderness portion of the Snake River Plain still retains that look of apocalypse. But in too many places, the river itself has been drastically changed by the hand of man. The main stem of the Snake is now chained by a score of dams, from Jackson Lake in Wyoming to Ice

Balanced Rock, a weathered chunk of lava 40 feet high, defies wind and gravity on a bluff above Salmon Falls Creek Canyon, Idaho.

Harbor Dam near the confluence with the Columbia. Almost two fifths of the river's once raging course already lies beneath the deep, still waters of the reservoirs, and the demands of civilization for hydroelectric power continually increase. There are plans for more dams, more reservoirs, more dead water. An extraordinary map, published by the U.S. Army Corps of Engineers a few years back, shows all of the dams and reservoirs that already exist or are contemplated for Snake River country. On the map the Snake appears as an unbroken series of reservoirs from where it joins the Columbia all the way back upstream to the head of Brownlee Reservoir. The map shows other reservoirs covering mile after mile of the Snake's tributary streams: the Salmon, the Clearwater, the Selway, the Lochsa. Not all of these dams have been built and hopefully some of them never will be, but there is something frightening about an attitude of mind that can calmly contemplate the vast scheme depicted by the map.

Yet a few free-running stretches of the Snake remain—in the Tetons, where the river twists in long graceful oxbows below the mountain wall; in the precipitous, turbulent Mad Canyon, where Wilson Price Hunt first saw it; and especially along the Idaho-Oregon line, where the river enters its stupendous gorge, Hells Canyon.

Of these gorges, Hells Canyon is by far the deepest. The vertical distance from the rim of the bordering ranges to the surface of the river averages 5,500 feet—deeper than the Grand Canyon. Unlike the Grand Canyon, where a man on the river can often see the highest part of the rim above, here the lower shoulders of the mountains generally block their summits from view; only rarely, coming around a bend in the river, can one glimpse the true height of the land above, and the eye is shocked by the sensation of depth.

A raft trip through Hells Canyon begins a few miles upstream from Wild Sheep, the first bad rapids. We reached our raft-launching point via a twisting road that led from Cambridge, Idaho, and paralleled the river's course. This approach is not an encouraging prelude to a wilderness trip. Along a hundred miles of the canyon the river is drowned beneath a string of three long, flat reservoirs. We passed Brownlee, a lake surrounded by a border of raw rock and gravel—the ugly bathtub ring left behind whenever water is drawn down. We passed Oxbow Reservoir, the dam end crowded with flotsam, and finally arrived at Hells Canyon Reservoir, where armadas of carp cruised the slack water.

Campbell pulled off the road at a turnout, and we stopped to stretch.

Campbell looked down into the gorge and said, "Before these three dams this was the greatest stretch of the river. In this flooded section the river dropped ten feet a mile, and there were huge rapids every half mile. It was the best white water in the United States, better even than the Grand Canyon." The words came out sour. Campbell runs the river commercially, carrying paying tourists in his rafts, but he's an uncommon entrepreneur. I think if he felt it would save the river from development he'd give up running it entirely and leave it to the sturgeon and the mergansers.

Of the new dams that have been proposed for Hells Canyon, one, the Pacific Northwest Power Company's High Mountain Sheep Dam, would be 670 feet high and would put another 58 miles of the canyon under water. Only a prolonged war waged by conservation groups has kept High Mountain Sheep and the others from becoming realities.

We drove on, passing miles more of reservoir, most of it apparently uninhabited by much of anything—certainly uninhabited by the swarms of happy people who, we are told by various dam builders, are drawn like bees to honey by the recreational benefits of such still-water reservoirs. They must all have been at Disneyland. Finally we reached the great concrete slab of Hells Canyon Dam, standing 395 feet above the river, where we were greeted by a cheerful sign emplaced by the Idaho Power and Light Company: "This place really turns me on."

Never mind. The stretch below us was 110 miles of raw, wild river, and as we prepared the rafts and made ready to launch we could hear the thunder of water down below.

I found it a strange, surreal voyage, drifting down the black water between Hells Canyon's walls. The landscape would have delighted 19th Century artists who saw the West in romantically florid terms and portrayed it with the exaggeration of a fun-house mirror. Hells Canyon—I could imagine the painting, with blood-red water flowing through a coal-black chasm so steep and sheer that overhead only a narrow sliver of sky might be visible. The canyon is not like that, but the twisting river is dark and narrow and very deep. Above, the basalt cliffs of the ancient lava flows rise for some 2,000 feet. And above and beyond them the mountains reach away, covered with grass that was pale at this early season, so that the occasional high peaks that one could perceive from the canyon looked soft and gently sculptured, as if covered with thick green velvet.

As we traversed the boils and narrow guts of that first 20 miles below Hells Canyon Dam and careered through the big rapids—Wild

A 50-foot-high palisade of basalt, a lava flow hardened into vertical columns, rises from the plains near Boise, Idaho.

Sheep, Granite Creek, Waterspout—it seemed incredible that men ever ran this river in really large ships. But they did—twice. For a brief time after the Civil War, a stern-wheeled steamboat, the *Shoshone,* had worked the river above the canyon. But demand for her services dwindled, and she was left rotting on the riverbanks until 1869, when her owners conceived the extraordinary idea that she could be brought through Hells Canyon to Lewiston and used on the lower river. They sent a Captain Sebastian Miller after her with orders to bring her through or wreck her in the attempt. Miller must have been a man of vast skill and monumental hubris. With a small crew he made the *Shoshone* seaworthy and took off downstream, running his engines in reverse to hold her back in the rushing current.

It was some boat ride. The *Shoshone* hung up in whirlpools and spun like a carrousel, sideswiped rocks, smashed eight feet of her bow, broke her stern wheel to pieces, and shipped so much water that the firemen were driven from the boiler deck. But she made it through, and when it was all over Miller told his engineer, "Buck, I expect if this company wanted a couple of men to take a steamboat through hell, they would send for you and me."

On the lower Snake and on the Columbia and Willamette rivers the *Shoshone* put in four working years before, ironically, she hit a rock in a stretch of placid water and sank. Her cabin was ultimately resurrected as a chicken coop.

Twenty-one years later, a Captain William Gray tried the same thing with another stern-wheeler, the *Norma.* Gray, a dour-looking, squinty-eyed man of extraordinary daring, used to test rapids by swimming through them. Mindful of Captain Miller's experience with his caved-in bow, Gray stuffed his hull with cordwood to absorb the impact when he caromed off rocks, and stood nervelessly at the wheel while the boat shot downstream at 20 miles per hour. Gray sideswiped a lot of real estate and terrified his crew, but he brought the *Norma* through. In the process her hull was knocked full of holes, into which the men stuffed stovepipes to help bail out all the water she'd shipped. By the time she reached Lewiston she bristled with so many stovepipes "she looked like a gunboat that had been in a hard battle."

For three days we floated the river by raft. From time to time we stopped along the banks to look at places where Indians had dwelled as long as 8,000 years ago—many centuries before the coming of the tribes we know today. Small bands of these prehistoric people probably sought out the canyon during winter, when the river-level climate is much milder than that of the mountains above. There are some 200 of these archeological sites in the unflooded portion of the canyon; God knows how many lie beneath the reservoirs. To the layman they speak in a subtle voice—here a brush-covered depression in the earth where the winter lodges stood; there, on a rock face overhanging the river, a tracery of ocher representing . . . a man? an elk? You are sure only that someone has been here, long, long before you.

At lunch stops we fished for the smallmouth bass that abound in the wild portion of the river. Strong, beautiful bronze-colored acrobats, they charged out from steep rocky ledges to savage our lures, then came up out of the water on their tails, Nijinskys of fish. Twenty-four other species live in the wild river. One night at camp, with more hope than sense, we baited a huge hook with bass heads and set it out to catch the greatest Snake River fish of all, the white sturgeon. These leviathans, armored with overlapping ridges of bony plate, are relics of prehistory; their direct forebears swam the seas 300 million years ago. They are among the largest fresh-water fish in the world: one caught in the Snake River in 1898 was 12 feet long and weighed in the neighborhood of 1,500 pounds.

Sturgeon may live to be 100 years old, and they are prodigious reproducers—a single female may deposit two to three million eggs. Yet even with this capacity for procreation, the species is in a precarious state. What eons of competition and predation had failed to do, the dams have done in a few years. The sturgeon can live only in the deep holes of the wild river and apparently are unable to survive the environment of the still-water reservoirs. Hells Canyon is one of the few remaining spots where one can fish for them; and I wanted to hook one (but not to kill him; by Idaho law any sturgeon caught must be returned unharmed to the river) because there is something about the sturgeon that tugs at the caveman in me. I wanted to feel the deep-throbbing line and the sense of being locked in combat with a creature older than the dinosaurs. But no sturgeon came to our bait. These fish did not last millions of years by being pushovers.

Later that night we sat and yarned around a campfire of mountain mahogany. Campbell talked about the problems of the river runner: campsites were getting more and more difficult to find because the river dropped its load of sediment behind the dams and could no longer replenish its natural sand beaches. These beaches were washing away at the rate of 20 per cent a year, and some had already turned to bare rock. Quota systems, now being established for the use of such other white-water rivers as the Colorado, were prompting more and more people to come to the Snake.

"It's an exponential thing," Campbell said. "This year there'll be a three to four hundred per cent increase in usage over last year. There's not enough firewood, not enough campsites, problems with sanitation —there's no way the river can stand it."

With more and more rafts on the river and more jet boats—big craft that can blast through heavy rapids on shafts of water thrust through a jet water pump powered by a diesel engine—the danger of serious accidents was growing. There had been none so far, but everyone was aware of the fact that a jet boat running upstream and a raft running down might well be committed to a collision course: their crews would be unable to see each other until too late. The Forest Service had pondered the problem, but nobody really knew what could or should be done. The river is layered with overlapping jurisdictions—three state governments, the Coast Guard, which functions here to regulate boating safety, and the Forest Service were all involved. It was not clear just who was in charge here.

We watched the fire, listened to the surge of the river in its banks and finally went to our sleeping bags. Dazzled by stars, I lay awake for a while. The night was so crystalline that up above I could see, for one of the very few times in my life, all the faint stars of the Little Dipper. At the end of the Dipper's handle hung Polaris, the star of the explorers. A steady white beacon, it drew me toward sleep.

The Crags' Harsh Beauty

PHOTOGRAPHED BY JAY MAISEL

Of all the Snake River country's remote fastnesses, few remain as untouched as the Crags, a dramatic line of glacier-carved peaks at the northwest edge of the Selway-Bitterroot Wilderness. Men seldom visit this granitic palisade, 8,000 feet high and snowbound from November to June. The Crags in winter hold little game —an occasional mountain goat traversing the razorback ridges, or an elk in the meadows. Most of the year the area is inhabited chiefly by rodents that live in its valleys.

Moreover, there are none of the minerals that tempt prospectors. For hikers, only a few Forest Service fire-control trails, originally cut in the early 1900s, thread through the passes and up the rugged slopes. These trails are not for Sunday excursionists: sometimes they plunge at a 50° angle along narrow ridges littered with loose rock debris.

Yet for a trail-wise and discerning visitor, the Crags present a fascinating spectrum of the subtle yet profound interactions between rock masses and plants in a harsh subalpine environment. For thousands of years, plants here have maintained a slow, root-against-rock assault on the heights. Inch by inch and year by year they have moved onto slopes and into vales once barren of life.

These plants of the high country must be able to take root in the thinnest of soils, and survive subzero winter winds and desiccating summer sun. The growing season lasts but two short months, into which the plants must cram their seeding and most of their manufacture of food reserves for the whole year.

The largest of the trees—the alpine firs—anchor themselves with long, strong roots. And they conserve energy by renewing only a portion of their leaves each year. Shrubs like the wild rose and fool's huckleberry have woody stems that preserve moisture despite drying winds; these stems also store carbohydrates for winter food. Sedges and grasses hug the ground, bend with the breeze and die down to their subterranean stem-tips each autumn.

By September, the month when these photographs were taken, temperatures as low as 25° have helped to turn the sedges brown. Fool's huckleberry and heather ripen their seeds in pentagonal capsules of a rusty beige while alpine firs loose theirs on filmy wings. And all the perennial plants have increased the frost-resistant sugars in their cells essential for the eight-month winter.

Inside a small, round valley scooped out by a glacier, firs and shrubs partly enclose a tarn, blanketing terraces (left) and creeping up toward the tops of the Crags. Even the steep talus slopes of loose rock rubble are dotted with fir and lower-growing plants like the alpine knotweed (foreground).

Base Camps of the Growing Things

The base camps of the encroaching plants are the 4,000-foot-high valleys. Here, soil and water can accumulate on a relatively flat floor and gently curving lower slopes. Mountain walls provide some protection from sun and winds. Snows, up to 14 feet deep, insulate some plants against subzero winds and create a reservoir of water for release in spring and into the dry summer.

A single valley may offer dozens of examples of how the plants in a typical subalpine environment are adapted to varying combinations of soil and water. The thinnest accumulations of soil may support mosses, thickets of shrubs and small groves of alpine fir. At the valley's center, where soil lies deeper, water-loving willows and sedges emerge on banks of small streams and lakelets. Where the snow melts slowly —beneath trees or in the shade of the surrounding mountains—a shrub like Trapper's Tea may flourish, spreading leaves that once provided mountain men with a tangy brew. In more open areas, where snow melts quickly, bracken fern and grouseberry sprout from the drier ground. On steep slopes, where meltwater sweeps away swiftly, only the tenacious fir and lichen can survive.

A valley's floor and its gently sloping walls display a closely woven autumnal tapestry. Deep green firs and lighter green Trapper's Tea set off the red-orange of grouseberry and the russet tones of the sedges and grasses.

Bracken fern hoards water during the
few moist days of spring to sustain
itself through the arid summer. Here,
drying out in the fall, the ferns
turn brassy yellow and copper orange.

Sun-gilded lichens hang from fir
boughs touched with the orange glow
of dead needles. On the ground, red-
leafed wild rose mingles with
yellowing fool's huckleberry. This
shaded valley vegetation clusters
thickly in the spare soil, watered by
seepage from melting snowbanks.

First a Foothold, Then a Small Domain

Higher on the flanks of the Crags, where the granitic skeleton shows through, there are few places for snow to linger or soil to form. Plants must advance like skirmishers, taking advantage of every crack and shelf, dip and hollow.

In the van, as always, is the alpine fir, clinging to slopes too steep and barren to support any other life but rock-hugging lichens. Other species almost always follow. Heat, frost and acids, formed by lichens and tree roots, crack and chip rocks, creating crevices and minute bits of new soil for mosses, grasses and sedges. Slowly, these plants gather rock particles, dust and decayed matter around them until an alpine knotweed or a grouseberry bush can take root. Each year the new plants extend their domain, trapping a few more particles, and forming a bed to hold a little more water.

This slow conquest is sometimes checked, but never stifled. Fire caused by summer lightning may erase a century's accumulation of undergrowth, leaving charred ranks of firs to weather into gray ghosts. Yet, inevitably, spring winds and meltwater will bring seeds, and new herbs, shrubs and trees will germinate and recloak the bare rock.

Ledges of bedrock thrust through a field of boulders dumped on a mountain shelf by retreating glaciers. Between the stones, wispy brown elk sedge and foot-high ruddy-leaved grouseberry bushes have spread into every available crack and crevice.

Firs cling to the crevices and shallow
shelves on the precipitous face of a
crag amid swirling mists that creep up
along gullies gouged out by glaciers
and enlarged by years of weathering.

Alpine plants trace in green a network
of fissures covering this glacier-honed
peak. The plants root in cracks
widened almost imperceptibly each
year by frost action and root growth.

The gaunt gray trunks of firs mark the aftermath of a fire that swept across the Crags a dozen years earlier. In the dry mountain air, where wood rots slowly, the dead trees will probably stand for decades. Shrubs have crept back among the rocks; before the last trunk falls, a green wave of young firs will have regained the summit.

2/ The Buffalo Road

...the sounds, the colors, the cold, the darkness,
the emptiness, the bleakness, the beauty. Till
they died this stream of memory would set them apart.
...For they had crossed the continent and come
back, the first of all.   BERNARD DE VOTO/ THE COURSE OF EMPIRE

On a warm September afternoon we left the car on the old logging road
and climbed up Sherman Peak, a rise of land to our south. The mountainside was bright with color: deep green of heather and searing reds
and oranges of huckleberry. The country lay open, with stunted firs
here and there, hardly taller than a man, and lodgepole pines, hunchbacked, bent down by winter snows. The climb was not steep but the
weather was hot and we sweated and panted a little; I was glad to
come out onto the top and stand in the cooling wind.

A blue haze hung in the air; the season had been bad for fires and
now, in September, you could smell smoke everywhere in the northern
mountains. To the east rose the polished granite of the Bitterroots; to
the south the dinosaur-back of the Selway Crags and the steep-gullied
north faces above the Lochsa River. The air was full of swarming ladybugs; their faint buzzing sound lay lightly on the silence.

A granite outcropping stuck up a few feet above the summit. My
mind was on a couple of men who had come this way before me. They
had stood there, no doubt about that, anyone would have. I walked up
onto it, right to the top, and planted my feet exactly where theirs must
have been. I stood there for a long time, eyes half closed, and I could
see them—they have inhabited the corners of my mind for many years
and it was easy to see them. They came to this spot a day apart but in

my mind I saw them together, Lewis stumping along on his bowlegs,
Clark with his hair flaming like fire, coming slowly up the track, limping, leading their limping horses. Their rude clothes were in tatters,
their eyes fierce and red and sunken, their faces taut with hunger, so
close to exhaustion, so nearly broken, so tough.

This was the spot. When they stood on this outcropping where I now
stood, they must have known. During those weeks of hunger when
their meals were chokecherries and the flesh of their horses, during the
snow and sleet storms, during the long miles of trail so steep and rocky
that the horses went slipping and rolling down the mountainsides, even
indomitable as they were they must have doubted, must have wondered. But here on this outcropping their mood would have suddenly
changed. For, turning to the west, I could look out across the mad jumble of mountains and I could see, faintly through the haze of smoke, a
lightness—the broad slash of the Weippe prairie. The end of the mountains. They saw that same pale line below the pine-dark ridges, and
then they knew that they were going to make it.

Near the northern edge of the Snake River country, along a hogback
of broken ridges that stands above the Clearwater River and its tributary, the Lochsa, lies the Lolo Trail. The name of the trail derives,
most likely, from an Indian corruption of the name of one Lawrence, a
trapper (a more charming but probably far-fetched theory is that it was
named in honor of Lola Montez). The Lolo existed as a trail long before
the coming of the white men. The route was the Indians' buffalo road,
which the Nez Percé hunting parties followed year after year from
their home in the Snake River country down to the game-rich Montana
plains. Today, by tracing one's way through a 100-mile labyrinth of
dusty, winding, steep one-lane logging roads, a traveler can follow the
approximate and, sometimes, the precise route of the old Lolo Trail
and thus follow in the footsteps of the route's first white travelers, for
whom it was the vital link in the greatest journey of exploration in our
history. The Lolo is the trail of Meriwether Lewis and William Clark
and the Corps of Discovery.

In this eighth decade of the 20th Century, a child may still dream of
growing up to be the greatest President of the United States or the greatest scientist, or the greatest industrialist or the greatest general. But it is
not possible to dream of being the greatest explorer, for the job was
filled long ago and few employment opportunities remain in that line of
work. Lewis and Clark were the first men to cross the piece of real estate
that is now the United States. At the time of their crossing, white men

had already penetrated some distance eastward up the Columbia from the Pacific, and the great Alexander Mackenzie had reached the West Coast by a journey across Canada. But no white had ever seen the Snake River country. No one even knew it was there.

The most sophisticated conceptions of the West had failed even to guess at the width and scope of the Rocky Mountains and had posited a simple geography in which the Missouri River headed at a height of land no more than a short stroll from navigable water that led to the Pacific. Here the two explorers would find the Northwest Passage, with the slight inconvenience of a brief portage. In 1804 President Jefferson dispatched Lewis and Clark and their Corps of Discovery of 30-odd men to go up the Missouri, find the passage and continue on to the Pacific. Jefferson's intent was to establish a trade route to the Far East; to secure a piece of the rich northwestern fur trade; and perhaps most important, to establish a presence on the Pacific Coast of the continent that would one day secure the land beyond the mountains to the developing United States of America.

Insofar as Lewis and Clark accomplished this last objective, their exploration is probably the most significant in our history. They failed to accomplish the first, because, of course, there was no Northwest Passage, nothing even close to one. For in between the heads of navigation lay the peaks of western Montana and the Snake River country—a couple of hundred miles of high, rugged mountains, and rivers barely navigable to a chip of wood. It was here in the Snake River country that the going got rough and the obstacles became nearly insuperable, here that the key to the puzzle of the continental crossing had to be found. And it is here that the explorers' names live on. Each of the leaders has a town named in his honor (Lewiston, Idaho, and just across the Snake, Clarkston, Washington); each, a river (the Lewis River is a major tributary of the upper Snake—Clark's Fork, in Montana, flows to the Columbia by a route slightly north of the Snake's); each, a bird common to the region (Lewis' woodpecker and Clark's nutcracker); each, an entire genus of Western flora, with a half dozen or more individual species. Their names also appear these days on everything from motels to a locally popular brand of vodka.

It is here too, particularly on the Lolo Trail, that you can come close to sensing their presence—the hint of smoke on the wind might come from their not-far-distant campfire and then you know they passed this way, not 170 years ago but just a few hours, perhaps a day.

At another ridge about 160 miles southeast of Sherman Peak, on August 12, 1805, Meriwether Lewis, Captain, First Infantry, Commander of the Corps of Discovery, reached the Great Divide. He stopped there, breathing hard we can be sure, but not just from exertion. Lewis had reached the ridgepole of the continent and stood looking down the other side. Shortly before, Lewis and a small advance party (Clark, slowed down by a tumor on his ankle, rejoined his partner after five days) had come to the headwaters of a tiny stream, one of the uppermost tributaries of the Missouri River. There, Private Hugh McNeal had stood exultantly with one foot on each side of the stream and thanked God "that he had lived to bestride the mighty & heretofore deemed endless Missouri."

Now, as the party started down the far slope of the divide, Lewis found another small stream, where he stopped to drink the clear, cold water—and there was another moment of exultation. The water was running west, to the Pacific; the eastward-flowing stream that became the Missouri lay two miles back over the ridge: this was as close as man would ever come to finding the Northwest Passage.

On this day, for the first time, a white man entered the Snake River country. From the top of the divide, Lewis had seen "immence ranges of high mountains still to the West of us with their tops partially covered with snow." But perhaps because the day was triumphant, there is no hint in Lewis' journal that the sight of those mountains filled him with foreboding—although it should have.

If anyone could survive the rigors that lay ahead, these two young Army officers, Meriwether Lewis and William Clark, were the men. They were the most competent explorers in our history, perhaps in anyone's history. They crossed the continent and returned, having spent two and a half years in a howling wilderness populated by Indians and belligerent grizzly bears. They crossed some of the most savage territory the continent has to offer, territory that takes its toll of human lives to this day. In all those months and all those miles, they lost one man, who died, apparently, of appendicitis. And by and large they made it all look remarkably easy; the story of their trip is a chronicle of mistakes that were never made.

Lewis, only 29 at the start of the expedition and four years Clark's junior, was the nominal commander. But the two decided between themselves that they would share command, and they did—the kind of agreement that would normally result in chaos in any field of endeavor. Yet so perfectly did they make it work that in two and a half years there was never a significant dispute between them. Even after their return to civilization they remained steadfast friends until Lewis' untimely death in 1809 parted them.

The men complemented each other, Clark the yang to Lewis' yin. Both were experienced officers and frontiersmen, but there the similarity ended. Lewis, who had served as Jefferson's personal secretary, was the more sophisticated, the more polished. He was a young aristocrat, a visionary, full of poetry and a profound sense of his own destiny, and with a dark streak of melancholy in him. Just after crossing the Continental Divide he chastised himself in his diary for his failure to accomplish anything significant in his life. And his death, only three years after his return from the West, may have been suicide. Clark, the younger brother of the Revolutionary War General George Rogers Clark, seems more roughhewn; a natural leader of men, even-tempered, unflappable, humane, he had, in addition, an uncanny ability to read the lay of the land.

By the time Lewis and Clark reached the Continental Divide, they were 15 months out of Saint Louis. Already they had survived many adventures and had surmounted, by means of uncommon foresight, ingenuity and steadfastness, a host of obstacles. But the worst lay ahead in the climactic search for the route to the Pacific. The true path was somewhere to the west, in the tangle of mountains that makes up northern Idaho. But how to find it?

Lewis had crossed the divide at Lemhi Pass and started down the Lemhi River, a small tributary of the Salmon. He correctly assumed that the Lemhi was part of the Columbia River system, but neither he nor Clark had any concept of the size and difficulty of the country between them and the Columbia proper. When Clark rejoined him, the two explorers prepared to continue downstream, although Shoshone Indians whom they met warned them against it. The Indians claimed the big river into which the Lemhi flowed was impassable.

According to an entry in Lewis' journal, the Shoshone said that the "bed of the river was obstructed by sharp pointed rocks and the rapidity of the stream such that the whole surface of the river was beat into perfect foam as far as the eye could reach." The banks of the river, they added, were so perpendicular that there was no possibility of passing along the shore.

The Indians were, of course, describing the Salmon, the River of No Return. But the explorers decided to try anyway, and Clark with a

Bear grass blooms alongside the Lolo Trail in

stretch of high country west of the Bitterroot Mountains, whose rounded summits are sheathed in the haze of a quiet July afternoon.

small party set out on a reconnaissance. It took him just four days to find out that the Indians were right. Sick from a diet of chokecherries and red haws—all they had found to eat along the Salmon—Clark and his men retraced their steps to join Lewis. By now both of the officers had learned from Indians of another route across the mountains, some distance to the north of the raging Salmon. This was the Indians' buffalo road, the Lolo Trail.

Already, at the beginning of September, the Rocky Mountain winter was close at hand. All the same, the party, with 29 horses purchased from the Shoshone, started north—up the north fork of the Salmon, across the mountains and down to the Bitterroot River. They lost the trail, got pelted with sleet and snowstorms and struggled over "emence hills and some of the worst roads that ever horses passed." The animals slipped and fell frequently; one was crippled and two more simply gave out. There was no game and little else to eat. But they pushed ahead, and on September 11 they finally found the Lolo Trail and cut westward again.

Today only a couple of days are needed to travel the Lolo Trail, by pickup truck or car, and the only real worries are the possibilities of getting high-centered on a rock or of making the wrong turn in the maze of logging roads. I went over the trail, by car and a little shanks' mare, with a big gentle man named Andy Arvish, a Forest Service ranger who has spent years of his spare time bushwhacking through this steep and difficult country in an effort to trace the exact route of Lewis and Clark. Sometimes the route follows the logging roads, sometimes it diverges for many miles. Arvish has found most of the original trail, but some segments still elude him, and the search for them will occupy him for some time to come. The trail is still visible in places, he explained, because it was originally a network of game trails and the animals have continued using the route to this day.

Even traveling the trail as comfortably as we did, I felt a growing respect for the explorers' fortitude. Once, as we stood looking down from a ridge at the sweep of the Bitterroots, Andy said, "You look out there at the jumble of drainages and think, 'Which the hell way is down?'"

Which way indeed? The mountain architecture here seems totally random, thrown down, a freehand drawing by a bad artist. The geography has no logic. Creeks run off in all directions to join other creeks running off in all directions. Ridgelines wander here and there so that a traveler must go up, then down, then up again, and the shortest distance between two points is a long way around.

For two days we poked along the dusty logging roads. At night we camped in a grove of spirelike firs, and in the morning all around our camp were deer tracks—something the explorers would have envied.

The country is not particularly beautiful, for it has been heavily logged and the mountains are flayed-looking and veined with logging roads. But along the trail itself, people like Andy have kept the loggers at bay. From time to time we would leave the road and hike out into the woods until we struck the old trail, and then we would follow it for a while. The experience was a little eerie. The trail was just a faint trace, so indistinct that, while Andy seemed to know exactly where he was going, I sometimes could not tell that we were on any trail at all. The route was choked with windfalls, so crisscrossed with fallen logs that every few yards we had to clamber over them. To progress even a quarter mile seemed to take a long time. But back in the car, when I consulted the journals, I found that Clark, hungry and exhausted, had by his own reckoning made as much as 32 miles per day over this same ground.

As I said, they were tough.

You can get a feeling from the journals. "Much fatigued, and horses much more so," Clark wrote on September 15. "Several horses sliped and roled down steep hills, which hurt them verry much. The one which carried my desk & small trunk turned over and roled down a mountain for 40 yards & lodged against a tree, broke the desk."

The only wild game they found was a pair of grouse, and no water on the trail. They melted snow to drink and ate a colt for dinner.

Next morning snow started to fall before daylight and kept coming down all day. Clark went ahead to scout the trail but continually lost the way. Snow spilled down off the tree branches as the men passed, soaking them through. Clark had only thin moccasins and feared his feet were going to freeze. He saw some deer once, lined up his rifle on a buck, squeezed the trigger. The hammer snapped, nothing happened. He tried again. Misfire again. Once more. Misfire. He shot seven times and the gun never fired; the deer escaped. That night they killed and ate another colt.

The following day they could not find the horses until noon; the beasts had strayed for miles trying to find forage. The weather warmed and the snow began to melt, and they sloshed through mud and water. The trail was steep and slippery, and the horses had great difficulty making their way. Someone spotted a bear, which got away. They killed another colt for dinner. In the distance they could hear wolves howling.

And so the journey went. The men broke out in boils and grew weak from dysentery. Lewis' party was reduced to eating a coyote and a crow. One night Clark's advance group had nothing at all to eat. They named their campsite Hungery Creek and pressed on.

On the 19th, Lewis reached the top of Sherman Peak, the hill where I'd found the ladybugs swarming, and saw, to his "inexpressible joy," the prairie lying to the west. Sergeant Patrick Gass, the carpenter of the expedition, wrote in his journal: "When this discovery was made there was as much joy and rejoicing among the corps, as happens among passengers at sea who have experienced a dangerous protracted voyage, when they first discover land on the long looked for coast."

The corps had 40 hard miles to go before reaching the plain, but it was all downhill now.

Clark came down from the mountains first, on September 20, and was no sooner on the prairie than he spotted three small Indian boys, who ran in fright. Clark left his gun behind, went forward and found a couple of the children. He gave them some bits of ribbon as a token of good will. The boys then led him to their village, where the people at first were frightened of these half-starved apparitions from over the mountains. But the villagers proved to be kindly, and began to produce buffalo meat and salmon and berries and camas root. To Clark and his men it was a real feast.

The encounter proved historic, for this was the first contact, on the Indians' home ground, between white men and the tribe that came to be known as the Nez Percé. The Nez Percé, named by French-Canadian trappers for their pierced noses, were the lords of the northern Snake River country and they quickly became Clark's favorite Indians—as they have been just about everyone's favorite Indians ever since. They made superb bows, of horn backed with sinew, and were expert in their use. After they got firearms, they became renowned as sharpshooters. In addition, the Nez Percé were splendid horsemen. They had discovered the principles of selective breeding, and used their knowledge to develop the magnificent spotted horse that today is called the Appaloosa. The women were comely—a fact not lost on the members of the Corps of Discovery—and the men were peace-loving and honest. Lewis and Clark dealt fairly with them, as they dealt fairly with all Indians who could be dealt with at all, and the Nez Percé never forgot it. For 72 years after that first meeting with Clark in 1805, they did not raise a hand in violence against the white men who chivvied them

about. And when they finally did fight back, it was only because they were being driven to a reservation from their lush Wallowa Valley.

The Nez Percé war of 1877 was one of the most inglorious chapters in the inglorious history of dealings between American Indians and white men. Certainly it was one of the most embarrassing engagements in the annals of the United States Army. Under the spiritual leadership of a chief named Thunder-Traveling-to-Loftier-Mountain-Heights (the whites knew him simply as Chief Joseph), several bands of Nez Percé tried to escape to Canada. For three months and 1,700 miles they made a fighting retreat that still stands as a classic of military maneuver. They outwitted and outfought a vastly superior force of regulars and volunteers, and were finally caught and surrounded only a few miles short of their goal, the Canadian border.

Chief Joseph, the brilliant leader of the Nez Percé, directs his warriors from the bow of a dugout as they push off on a raiding expedition in this engraving from an 1877 issue of Frank Leslie's Illustrated Newspaper.

Chief Joseph's speech of surrender is surely the most famous ever made by an Indian: "I am tired of fighting. Our chiefs are killed. . . . It is cold, and we have no blankets. The little children are freezing to death. My people, some of them, have run away to the hills and have no blankets, no food. No one knows where they are—perhaps freezing to death. I want to have time to look for my children, and see how many of them I can find. Maybe I shall find them among the dead. Hear me, my chiefs! I am tired. My heart is sick and sad. From where the sun now stands I will fight no more forever."

But in 1805, all that was far in the future. To Lewis and Clark's weary Corps of Discovery, the Nez Percé represented salvation. Though dysentery ran through the expedition (perhaps as a result of sharing the Indians' diet), the men were saved from starvation, and able to rest enough to push ahead once more. When they reached the Clearwater River they were on navigable water once more, after a month and a half of difficult overland travel. On the Clearwater they found trees of a size that could be made into dugout canoes. They then launched themselves down the Clearwater to the Snake, down the Snake to the Columbia, and on the Columbia toward the ocean, with the friendly Nez Percé as their guides. They were in good hands.

At the western end of the Lolo Trail, near the point at which the Corps of Discovery emerged from the mountains, there stands today a tract of virgin timber preserved by the Forest Service as a memorial to the explorers. Clark camped here, and Lewis, passing by later, was impressed by the size of the trees. Always thinking ahead, he noted that they would have been big enough to make canoes.

On our trip over the trail, Arvish and I stopped and walked a way into the grove. It was a lovely place, cool and green, with occasional spears of sunlight shafting down through the canopy and spotlighting clumps of bright fern on the forest floor. We crossed over a glass-clear brook on a mossy log, and in a short while came to a huge white pine, the largest I have ever seen. Its trunk, almost as thick as I am tall, rose as straight and unbroken as a schooner's mast; the bark was gray and textured and unblemished, and the tree was so tall I had to tilt my head back to see the lowermost branches. It is called Clark's Tree, and we stood for quite a while admiring it, conscious of the fact that it had been standing right here, no doubt a big tree even then, when the explorers passed.

As we started back down the trail my eye caught some irregularity in the shape of a tree ahead, and I paused. Large, soft and brown, a form perched motionless on a branch next to the trunk. When the top of the object swiveled smoothly, I saw that it was a barred owl, a very big one. He was quite close, and because of the slope of the trail he was at about my level, but seemed unafraid. His feathers were thick and beautifully mottled; saucer-shaped disks on his face accentuated his eyes, which were large and dark and liquid, and almond shaped, like those of a Burmese dancer.

I stood, watching. I love watching owls because they watch back; they confront you with their presence. With his straight-eyed stare, unique among birds, the owl looked wise as a monk. I enjoyed a fantasy, for a moment, that some owlish ancestor had sat on the same branch those eight score years ago and watched the procession of men and horses passing beneath, and in an owl's wisdom had known that something new and different had come to his far mountains.

The owl and I regarded each other, amicably and with mutual curiosity. As the moments passed, the wild creature, the place and its association with great explorers made me think of a stanza from Stephen Vincent Benét that has always haunted me: "When Daniel Boone goes by, at night,/ The phantom deer arise/ And all lost, wild America/ Is burning in their eyes."

After a bit I started back down the trail. When I stopped to look back I saw that the owl had rotated the turret of his head so that he could continue watching me. I knew that he would watch me until I was out of sight.

A Moonscape on Earth

Within the last 100,000 years, in a remote part of what was to become south-central Idaho, the earth burst open and spilled millions of tons of lava over the Snake River plain, already ravaged by volcanic turmoil over the previous five million years. During these latest eruptions, three successive surges of molten rock flowed out over the land, cascading down hills, killing the trees, carrying off fragments of crater walls and dropping them miles away. Boiling lava spouted from vents, congealed in midair and fell back in profuse cinder showers, building cones that thrust to the sky. Steam and other trapped gases hissed from the hillsides in scalding clouds, while new vents opened on the flanks of old cinder cones and poured out fresh masses of incandescent magma.

Gradually, over the millennia, nature banked the subterranean fires. The last substantial eruptions here subsided about 2,000 years ago, cooling on the surface of a land that was now an eerie and alien waste more suggestive of the barren surface of the moon than of any place on earth. Today 83 square miles of this stretch of seared ground have been set aside as the aptly named Craters of the Moon National Monument.

None of the Far West's early explorers ventured into this forbidding landscape . The rough, broken surface made it impassable to horse or wagon, and the sun beating on the blackened surface drove off the hardiest footsloggers. Even the Indians rarely entered the area, though a faint trail and stone artifacts suggest that prehistoric tribes may have hunted small game or taken temporary refuge from their enemies there. Later tribesmen were also at some pains to avoid entering the region —possibly because vulcanism is a slow-dying process and there may have been lingering activity in the area. In 1879, an Indian told a local stockman that his great-great-great-grandfather had seen fire burning there. This, however, may have been merely vapor from escaping gases.

Craters of the Moon is still an empty and somewhat frightening place. A sparse cover of bushes and scrub trees grows in the crumbled lava as the plants slowly gain a foothold in the sparse soil, spreading their roots widely and spacing themselves to share the scant moisture. For the most part, however, the area remains a devastated pocket of wilderness—the terrestrial image of a dead satellite.

A yawning hole in Trench Mortar Flat bears witness to the devastation wrought by the lava flows that once inundated the Craters of the Moon region. Trench Mortar Flat is studded with such formations, whose resemblance to Civil War mortars gives this portion of the National Monument its name. These features, known to geologists as tree molds, were created as lava engulfed a tree, charring its trunk. Eventually the tree crumbled away, leaving its shape cast in lava.

A gigantic volcanic hole yawns 200 feet
deep, 660 feet wide and 2,000 feet in
circumference, the most awesome
cavity in a chain of craters that extends
in a northwest-to-southeast slash
across the entire National Monument.

The summit of Big Cinder Butte, tallest
cone in the area, rises 800 feet above
the plain. Limber pines, Douglas fir and
aspen find a foothold in the cone's
cinders; syringa and tansy bushes
flourish on the lava in the foreground.

A growth of dwarf buckwheat, evenly spaced by competition for nutrients, speckles a cinder field on the southeastern side of Inferno Cone.

A congealed river of lava, its surface cracked in cooling, cuts a broad downhill bed across the eroded remains of earlier eruptions.

Lava remnants took on these tortured shapes after frost action split the volcanic rubble.

Lichen dots a cracked "breadcrust bomb," a lava clot solidified in air during eruption.

Bright clusters of a plant called rubber rabbitbrush, which contains tiny amounts of rubber, bloom on the slope of a cinder cone. Typical of the hardy vegetation in Craters of the Moon Monument, the rabbitbrush has put down its roots in lava cinders enriched by airborne dust and sprinkled by a sparse 17 inches of annual rain.

3/ Fire in the Big Woods

The forests of America, however slighted by man, must have been a great delight to God; for they were the best he ever planted.   JOHN MUIR/ THE AMERICAN FORESTS

We dismounted and led the horses for the last five miles down Moose Creek. A long ride downhill on a bad trail can be agony for someone whose body is not accustomed to it. The flesh on the inside of my knees was red and tender, and my ankle ached from the mare's kicking me the day before. But even with the ache, things had reached a point for me where anything was better than riding any farther, and so I just limped slowly along the trail, so happy at being off the ponderous, bone-jarring animal that the hurt in my ankle felt almost pleasurable. John Meyer—a guide and packer—and I were traveling through the largest legally designated Wilderness in the United States, the 1,250,000-acre Selway-Bitterroot Wilderness in northern Idaho. Named for the Selway River, which drains the country, and for the Bitterroot Range, which bounds it on the east, the Selway-Bitterroot stretches out in a horizon-wide sweep of mountains, dense forest, and brushy sidehills browsed by enormous bands of elk. The area contains virtually no roads and the 1,000 or so miles of trail are woefully steep and overgrown.

People can disappear in the Selway-Bitterroot. Back in the 1940s a wild man lived in the mountains, breaking into Forest Service lookout towers to steal food, and filching clothing from the laundry lines of ranches on the perimeter. The man became known as the Human Coyote of the Selway and he was able to elude his pursuers for years before the law finally caught up with him.

A good enough woodsman could probably pull the same stunt today, for the Selway-Bitterroot is one of the few places left where someone who wants to go into the woods and be alone can really do it. In the 24 hours since leaving the roadhead on the Bitterroot Divide we had seen only a couple of backpackers. They stood aside for our pack string and looked at us with the unconcealed hostility of the hiker for horses, which make the trail dusty and litter it with manure.

Apart from a general yen for back-country exploration, I had some particular reasons for poking around in this northern part of the Snake River country. I wanted to make a sentimental journey to Crystal Peak, a mountaintop in the St. Joe National Forest where I'd spent a summer as a fire lookout 20 years before. I wanted to learn something about a new Forest Service plan to let some natural fires burn free in the forest. And I particularly wanted to see the place we were now heading toward, the Moose Creek Cedar Grove.

Most of the Snake River country lies in the rain shadow of the Pacific coastal ranges. Except for the ponderosa pine and an occasional tall fir, the trees are not especially large, nor are the woods particularly thick. But as the wilderness traveler moves north in Idaho, precipitation increases and the forests become denser. Once into the drainage of the Selway River, you are within the boundaries of a big woods that stretches all the way to the Canadian border and beyond. We had been riding in that woods for about 25 miles and now, just after I gave up straddling the horse and started to walk, we reached the magnificent old cedars I had come to see.

The Moose Creek grove is one of the most impressive stands of virgin western red cedar in the United States. For five miles the trail meandered between great trunks, eight or nine feet in diameter. The trunks were well spaced, columnar, the bark gray and delicately fluted. There was something about them that made me think of the stateliness and mass of elephants. Looking up, I saw that the trunks retained their bulk to a height of 70 or 80 feet, then tapered abruptly into crowns shaped like arrowheads. The feathery sprays of scalelike leaves so totally blocked the sun that the light in the forest had an eerie quality, as if passed through a green filter. Where the sun did find a gap, it struck through in long shafts, lighting a high haze of dust or pollen, so that the air itself seemed visible, tangible.

The wood from the cedar tree is unique, as anyone knows who has ever had the pure pleasure of splitting a chunk into kindling. Absolutely straight-grained and knot-free, it turns even the clumsiest

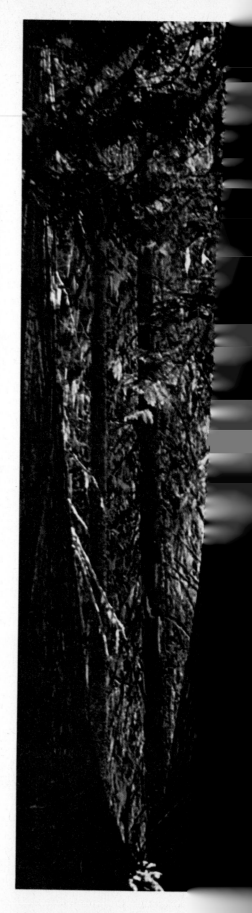

woodsman into a Paul Bunyan; the wood seems to fall apart at the touch of the ax. That easy workability and the capacity to withstand moisture made cedar wood especially attractive to Indians, who used it for making totem poles and for fashioning their dugout canoes—some of which, hewn out of a single log, were up to 65 feet long and could carry as many as 40 people.

Today the demand for cedar shingles has produced a thriving black market in cedar stolen from public lands. In the northern part of the Snake River country the cedar beasts, as the rustlers are called, patrol the forests with chain saws and covered pickup trucks, knocking down choice trees, sawing off enough shingle bolts to fill their trucks, and leaving the rest to rot.

We stopped for the night in the heart of the grove. John Meyer set up camp, while I wandered among the trees. Because of the dense shade there was no brush on the forest floor, no growth of young trees. The woods were open, like a park, and I could see for long distances between the trunks of the trees. The ground was covered with a mat of greenery, of lady fern and false Solomon's-seal, and a small plant I didn't recognize but which had tiny white flowers growing in pairs along its stems. Charmed by its delicacy, I picked one for a closer look. The flowers were so small that I could not see them well, even close up. I had no hand lens, and so I unscrewed one of the objective lenses from my binoculars and used it for a magnifier.

Under the glass I could see five tiny petals arranged in a star, with prominent yellow stamens and a swollen, outsized pistil. Magnified perhaps six times, the delicate flower was startling in its sexuality. The binocular lens was a new toy. In the failing evening light I walked around looking at things through it, peering at the lichens that encrusted the dead lower limbs of the trees, at mosses that covered fallen logs.

When I got back to camp John was making sheepherder's coffee —ground beans boiled in a pot—on a cedar fire. I'd tied a bit of bright red yarn to the end of my fishing-rod case to make it easier to spot. The case leaned against the bole of a huge cedar. Suddenly a thumb-sized hummingbird appeared from nowhere. The bird darted around the bit of yarn, thinking, apparently, that it was some bright flower full of nectar. Hovering there, with invisible wings making an audible hum, the bird flicked its stub tail, reminding me of a ballerina going up on points.

Finally, disappointed in the inability of the red yarn to produce dinner, the bird whisked up and perched on a branch. Seen against the

The autumn sun filters through a stand of western red cedars in Moose Creek Grove, in the heart of the Selway-Bitterroot Wilderness.

trunk of the tree, the bird was a tiny mote, almost lost against the gray elephant hide of the cedar—two living things close together for a moment, the one a million times larger than the other.

I wondered what the bird was doing there. The hummingbird's metabolism is so high it has to eat almost its weight every day. With no flowers save the tiny ones I'd seen, with nothing but the great looming hulks of the trees, how could it possibly find enough food? Perhaps it found flowers I overlooked, or filled out its diet with small insects.

Another puzzle had struck me earlier: beneath the heavy canopy there were no young trees, no cedar seedlings whatsoever. When these old trees died, would that simply be the end?

A few days later I would ask a botanist that question. Several possible explanations were being investigated, he said, but the answer was not yet certain. Perhaps fire or some other cataclysm was necessary to open up the forest to sunlight, so that the cedars could sprout. Cedars sometimes reproduce vegetatively. That is, if the branch of a living tree is forced to the ground by snow for some time, it may take root and generate a new seedling. But perhaps here the winter snows were not heavy enough to press the branches to the earth. Finally the botanist shrugged and said, "Maybe the tree has to wait for some shift in the region's climate before it can reproduce. Remember that the cedar only has to generate one successful seedling in its lifetime to perpetuate itself. And a cedar's lifetime is 800 years."

Dusk in the cedars. The green light in the forest had changed to green-gray, the trunks blending together in a fluted wall. The liquid call of a hermit thrush, far off. We sat at the campfire, John and I, and watched the flames. We talked campfire talk: the mules John had known, the bears I'd met. John is from the East, but the West had always tugged at his innards in a way he couldn't resist. He had thought about going to forestry school, but decided it would lead him to a job behind a desk, so he enrolled in a guides' school in Montana to learn from scratch those skills that mountain kids imbibe with their mother's milk.

In time, he had acquired the skills, and a feeling for the country as well. He said, "A friend of mine was down here once and he said 'There's a lot of God loose in this country.'" That is a statement that could sound sanctimonious, or corny, or both. But coming from this capable young fellow sitting next to me by the fire in the cedar grove, it seemed neither.

Night had come. Under the heavy canopy the sky was blotted out, the darkness complete. Using the flashlight, I walked down to the creek.

When I looked back, the tent had disappeared among the trees, blackness against blackness.

In this same cedar grove, perhaps at the same spot where our tent was now pitched, 30 men had camped more than 60 years before. They were firefighters, on a forced march into the Moose Creek country to put out a wildfire threatening the cedars. The spring of 1910 had been hot and dry, the fire season had started early, and by late August some 1,700 fires were burning in northern Idaho and adjacent areas of Montana and Washington. Thousands of men were in the woods trying to bring the fires under control.

On August 20th, the group of 30 camped at Moose Creek. The air was so full of smoke that it was pitch dark by 4 p.m. A hot wind came up from the southwest, and cedar needles fell like raindrops on their tents. The leader, a deputy forest supervisor named Ed Thenon, went to bed about 10 o'clock, but was roused out a little later by one of his men, who called, "I just saw a star fall on the hillside across the creek and it has started a fire." Thenon saw the little fire burning, saw a red glow to the west, and realized immediately that his man had seen no falling star. Burning embers were dropping out of the sky.

Thenon didn't know it, but he was caught in the middle of the largest forest fire in the history of the United States. High winds, which ultimately reached gale force, were uniting hundreds of small fires into solid walls of flame that would burn clear across northern Idaho.

Though ignorant of the fire's extent, Thenon did know he was in trouble. He roused his men and started a bucket brigade to wet down the driftwood and dead timber along the creekbanks. Then he covered the heads of the terrified horses with wet blankets, and made the men lie down in the shallow creek with other blankets over their heads. As the crown fire came raging in through the cedars from treetop to treetop, two of the crew went insane. It took three men to hold one of them down in the creek. The other, quite mad, danced about, sang lullabies—and miraculously escaped death while calling for his friends to throw water on him. As the fire enveloped them Thenon popped a bucket on his head, occasionally lifting it for air.

A few miles away one of Thenon's assistants was lying in another creek with his coattail over his head, surrounded by the floating bodies of hundreds of fish, probably killed by ash in the water. "Soon the velocity of the wind was so great," the man wrote later, "that unbelievably large pieces of burning bark, rotten wood and limbs were sailing through the sky ahead of the fire and falling everywhere. . . . Flames from the main fire were reaching out several hundred feet ahead of the fire and over the treetops. . . . The wind or draft from the fire was twisting off small trees and treetops. Big cedar trees seemed to explode from top to bottom as the fire advanced.''

Thenon and all his men survived. Elsewhere, others weren't so lucky. On Setzer Creek near Avery, Idaho, 28 men were burned to death; another 28 died on Big Creek off the St. Joe; eight suffocated east of Wallace. One ranger saved his panicky men by holding them in a creek at gunpoint. Ed Pulaski, another ranger, led his crew of 41 to safety in a deep mine tunnel. Thousands were saved by rescue trains that braved the flames and crossed burning trestles to evacuate people from threatened towns.

By the time heavy rains damped and then extinguished the fire, it had, within 48 hours, completely burned four towns, killed 85 people, and destroyed three million acres of forest.

Such tragedies have had a lot to do with attitudes toward forest fires. In the decades after 1910, the Forest Service worked zealously to develop techniques for suppressing all fire in the woods, and their efforts had full popular support. Many of us grew up with the indelible memory of the denizens of Bambi's forest fleeing in terror before the flames. The image of Smokey Bear, that stalwart figure with a hint of sadness in his brown eyes, is imprinted on us as totally as any symbol of our modern culture. Mountain lions and coyotes and hawks have always had their supporters, but wildfires are more like house rats —they have had no friends.

But today, fire has made some friends. In recent years, some forest ecologists, within both the Forest Service and the academic community, have started to speak up for fire. They see fire in the wilds not as a destructive aberration, but as merely one of the many natural forces that regulate the countryside. They believe that fire is often benign and sometimes absolutely essential.

Their heretical argument goes like this: the northern Rocky Mountains have always been fire country. Rain and snowfall are great enough to nurture forests, but most of the precipitation comes in winter as snow. The summers are hot and bone dry, with frequent thunderstorms that generate a great deal of lightning and very little rain. In this climate decomposition takes place very slowly. An acre of forest will deposit up to two tons of organic matter—leaves, needles, fallen branches—on the ground each year. No more than half of that is likely to decompose. The rest builds up, year after year, as potential fuel —the equivalent of 200 gallons of gasoline per acre.

When the inevitable lightning strike touches off this accumulated fuel, the result is apt to be wildfire on an apocalyptic scale. Over the centuries the environmental effects of such fires have been so complicated, and have had such subtle ramifications, that only in recent years have we begun to understand them. Fire has determined the kinds of plants that live in the Snake River country, the kinds of animals that live here, and their populations. For instance, the very survival of the lodgepole pines of the Snake River country depends upon fire. Their cones possess a characteristic known as serotiny—meaning that the scales are held so tightly by resin that they will not open to release seeds until they are superheated. After a wildfire the cones do open and within a few years the lodgepoles grow in dense thickets.

But lodgepoles in this region are short-lived trees, and at the age of a century or so they begin to lose the vigor that allows them to repel insects and disease. Today, after decades of fire suppression, the flats of the Tetons are a potential disaster area—mile after mile of mature lodgepoles are withering and dying from an infestation of the mountain pine beetle. Had occasional wildfires been allowed to burn, resulting in a mosaic of young and old trees, the spread of the infestation would have been checked naturally.

Animals, too, can benefit from forest fires. The elk that live in the mountains above the Selway, the Lochsa and the Clearwater rivers are magnificent animals. The big herd-bulls weigh half a ton and have antlers five feet across that resemble young trees. When running, the elk prance, lifting their legs high and holding their heads tilted back so that their huge racks can slip through the brush; they look proud as show horses. The large number of elk that inhabit northern Idaho is a direct result of the huge fire of 1910—and subsequent big burns in 1919 and 1934—which enriched the elk's diet. The elk live on a variety of low shrubs and grasses that cannot tolerate shade but that sprout up in profusion on burn scars where the tree canopy has been destroyed.

Today, after decades of effective forest-fire suppression, the great elk herds are decreasing at an alarming rate. The brushy mountainsides and old burn scars that are their natural habitat are giving way to continuous stretches of forest.

In the late '60s these facts—the diminishing herds, the accumulating fuel on the forest floor—began to bother some of the Forest Service's field researchers. In 1972, after two years of study, these men presented the Chief Forester in Washington with a careful proposal for a so-called free-fire zone, an area where lightning-caused fires would not necessarily be suppressed, but would simply be studied.

Washington approved the plan. The remote mountains of the Selway-Bitterroot Wilderness seemed a perfect place for such an experiment, and a 66,000-acre tract along White Cap Creek on the south side of the Wilderness was selected as a free-fire study area. In that first year, only one fire started on White Cap Creek. It burned an area 24 feet by 24 feet, and went out.

The payoff came a year later, on August 10, 1973. Lightning struck a medium-sized Douglas fir on Fitz Creek, a small tributary stream, and started a small blaze at the base of the tree. On the first day the Fitz Creek fire burned only three acres; a few men with shovels could easily have put it out. But the foresters made no effort to control the blaze. Instead they watched anxiously and hoped the fire would grow. It did.

On the second day the fire expanded only modestly, but on the third day it took off, roaring up the mountain through mixed stands of Douglas fir and ponderosa pine. The foresters wanted to keep the fire confined to the selected study area, but on the fifth day a tongue of flame crossed White Cap Creek and began to burn on the heavily forested slopes of the Snake Creek drainage to the south. Fanned by 20- and 30-mile-an-hour winds, the Snake Creek fire crowned—the flames began to leap from treetop to treetop, boiling 60 feet above the forest. The fire raced uphill at incredible speed, climbing 3,000 vertical feet from the creek bottom to the ridgetop in half an hour. This second fire, quickly dwarfing its parent blaze on Fitz Creek, seemed about to roar uncontrollably out of the study area; the Bitterroot Forest supervisor decided to suppress it. But the original fire was left to burn on.

When I went into the White Cap area on the 28th of August, a full 18 days after lightning had started the first blaze, the Snake Creek fire was dead after having burned over some 1,600 acres. The Fitz Creek fire had burned 1,000 acres before rain had knocked it down, but there still were sizable pockets of bright flame and columns of gray smoke dotted over the landscape.

For three days I hiked about in the burn with some companions from the Forest Service: Orville Daniels, the forest supervisor; and two of the young heretics who'd helped to create the free-fire zone—Dave

A natural fire ignited by lightning on a slope near Fitz Creek burns, unchecked, in an experiment to determine its benefit to the forest.

Aldrich, a fire specialist on Daniels' staff and Bob Mutch, a research forester with the Service's Missoula fire laboratory. I discovered, first of all, that the forest was far from dead, though it had died in places. Throughout much of the area, the fire had simply burned away the ground cover—the old litter of cones and needles, the low shrubs and grasses—with no harm at all to the trees themselves, which still looked green and healthy. In other large patches, the tree needles were singed to yellowish white and the trunks were charred, but even this did not mean that the country had been laid waste.

"The Douglas fir often will die after this kind of burning," Mutch said, "but it won't hurt the ponderosa pine at all. The bark is so thick and fire-resistant that the tree has to be practically burned through to kill it. The needles are all dead, but look here at these buds." He bent down a branch and showed me a healthy-looking green bud in the middle of the dead needles. "These buds will resist a lot of fire—next spring they'll refoliate the tree."

As we walked on through an area of bare, burned trees and scorched ground, Aldrich stopped by the remains of a small shrub with knobby-looking, deformed branches. "Do you see how this has been clubbed back? That's from overgrazing by elk. Next spring this burn will shoot up with dense young brush, and the elk will have a field day."

We glimpsed no elk, but many other animals had returned to the burn. We saw a black bear patrolling the edge of the fire area, and chipmunks running along burned logs. In the most devastated areas, blue grouse fed busily on fir and pine cones exposed by the fire. We couldn't tell whether they had been attracted by the roasted cones or whether the cones were more visible in the burned area.

One pocket of the Fitz Creek fire was still burning actively on a steep hillside, threatening to move outside of the study zone. We went down for a look, and Supervisor Orville Daniels decided to seal off the fire to prevent it from crossing the creek into the flammable area beyond. "If it goes past here," Bob Mutch said, "it's likely to take another couple of thousand acres, and we're not ready for that yet. It wouldn't really do that much harm, but a lot of people would be upset."

Bob started scratching a foot-wide line near the fire with the firefighter's basic weapon, a Pulaski, the combination ax and hoe invented by ranger Ed Pulaski, hero of the 1910 burn. I followed him, widening and deepening the line with a lady shovel—a small, short-handled digging tool with a sharpened blade. Bob and Dave had picked the downhill edge of the fire as the problem zone where we had to work. This choice surprised me, because forest fires tend to run uphill just as a flame goes up a matchstick held vertically above it. Bob pointed out that in high country, the upslope edge of a fire often burns into sparsely vegetated terrain and simply dies there from lack of fuel. In this steep country, paradoxically, the fire could also creep back downhill, even against strong winds, to burn the heavier timber of the creek bottom.

After a few minutes on the line I saw how this happened. A flaming ponderosa cone, fat and roly-poly as a softball, came bouncing downhill past me; it sailed right over our little shoestring fireline and into the dry brush below, where it immediately started a miniblaze of its own. Our fire could progressively roll such burning debris downslope until it reached the creek bottom; from there, it might jump the narrow stream and take off up the unburned opposite slope like a race horse.

Miserable work. My eyes watered from the smoke and my nose started to run. We tried to work as close to the burning edge as possible, in order to leave a minimum of unburned fuel between the control line and the flames. The big ponderosas just scorched and flamed superficially, but the dead limbs and fallen trunks blazed up so fiercely that I felt my skin searing whenever we had to work near them. Sometimes the heat became unbearable and we had to drop the line back.

On the hillside was a log, flaming at one end. A deer mouse, a nocturnal creature that is all big ears and glistening eyes, came darting out from under it. Though I stood only two or three feet away, the mouse ignored me completely and started running about in confusion. It could probably have got away, but fear of being out in broad daylight turned out to be greater than fear of the fire. After a moment the mouse shot back under the unburned portion of the log and disappeared. Ten minutes later, when I came back past that part of the line, I saw that the log now was burning along its entire length.

The fire proved to be more than we could handle. Flaming ponderosa cones, red-hot rocks and chunks of burning logs were rolling down slope and across the line everywhere, starting pockets of fire below us. In midafternoon a crew of full-time Forest Service smokechasers arrived to take over. Their leader, a big young man with eyes weary from the work of a long fire season, arrived at the line, shook his head, and said angrily, "I'd like to meet the son of a bitch who said we had to let this fire burn. I'd let him have one right in the nose."

Bob Mutch said nothing. He just looked at me and grinned.

The firefighter's anger was at the root of the problem that faces men

A fire-swept forest floor in the Crags section of the Selway-Bitterroot Wilderness shows the first signs of plant regrowth. With the tree

crowns burned off, increased amounts of sunlight have reached the ground, allowing low evergreens and red grouseberry to spring up.

like Mutch, who want to open large areas of our wilderness to natural fire. The Forest Service smokechasers are a proud elite of professional firefighters, and to many of these men the idea of letting fire run free is offensive if not downright insulting. The free-fire advocates must not only contend with such men, but also must convince a general public conditioned by years of Smokey Bear and all the other effective antifire propaganda. At the same time it must be remembered that Smokey has done an important job in making people vigilant against man-caused fires—a vigilance that should not be relaxed. For man-caused fires, because of the places they occur, can be especially destructive. Thus, though the free-fire advocates will have to teach people that wildfire is not necessarily evil, they must do so without diluting Smokey's basic message: be careful with cigarettes and campfires.

The problem will take more than a little solving, but the free-fire advocates are growing in number and voice. Partly as a result of the White Cap experiment, free-fire areas are being set aside in other National Forest wildernesses.

A few weeks later, back in the lookout's post on Crystal Peak after my absence of two decades, I stood by the fire finder—a rotating device equipped with sight vanes—and began to scan in a slow circle. The old familiar landmarks began to fall into place: Evergreen, Huckleberry, the bare stone outcropping of Lookout Mountain, Grandfather and Grandmother, Freezeout saddle (you can be sure that name cost somebody some pain), Anthony Peak, Flewsie Creek, Bechtel, Emerald Butte, St. Joe Baldy.

There they all were—the peaks and ridges and draws that a fire lookout, by season's end, knows the way a man knows the topography of his living room. Twenty years ago I'd known this terrain like that. Out from Ohio after my freshman year in college to work for the Forest Service in Idaho, I was so zonked by actually being in the Great West I'd dreamed about that I saw everything a little larger than life size. The mountains of my district were numbing in their beauty; my district ranger, heroic as Paul Bunyan. And in my job as a fire lookout I saw myself as something of a cross between Kit Carson and Gifford Pinchot, the great forester and conservationist. I grew long sideburns, tried to learn to shoot a pistol and saved up for a pair of $40 White logging boots with calks on the sole—the kind my district ranger wore.

And so here I was again, sideburns grayer, marksmanship still erratic and the White loggers somehow never purchased. My old cabin was gone, replaced by a 45-foot tower so the lookout could see over the surrounding trees—now taller by 20 years of additional growth. The country, with low, timbered mountains rolling away on all sides, was pretty enough, but not at all spectacular to someone who has seen the Tetons and the Sawtooths. The lookouts were a couple of nice kids, Bob and Carol Houghtaling, who do this every summer. The rest of the year they ramble around in their pickup camper, Bob playing his guitar and singing in bars and coffee houses when the money runs out.

We drank coffee and I played with the fire finder and tried to remember how you call in a smoke: "This is Crystal. I have a smoke in the northeast quarter of the southwest quarter, section 36, township 43 north, range 1 east, azimuth 170 degrees. Crystal clear."

We talked. I told them how, back in those prehistoric times, there was a war on porcupines here, because porcupines kill trees by eating their buds and the living cambium layer beneath the bark. In the ranger station we had a porky scoreboard, and every time you shot one you put a mark by your name. At the end of the season the district ranger treated the high scorer to a steak dinner. "We're still supposed to kill them, but we don't," Bob said. "Whenever a porcupine comes around here I just say, 'Please go away and quit gnawing on things because I don't want to kill you.'"

The idea appealed to me. I could see this whole new race of long-haired lookouts, disobeying orders and instead of killing the porcupines just having friendly conversations with them. Very civilized. Shouldn't there be enough trees so the porkies can have some too?

Later, Bob got out his guitar and played some of his own compositions. One of them delighted me, because it rang with the names of the surrounding mountains:

Huckleberry pie, Huckleberry pie.
I got it in my eye, for some Huckleberry pie.
Evergreen girl, Evergreen girl.
On top of the world, with my Evergreen girl!
Way up high on Crystal Mountain, any time of year,
Way up high on Crystal Mountain,
Life is Crystal clear!

I wanted to be alone with my own nostalgia, so in the afternoon I walked out on a rocky promontory where I used to go to meditate. I listened to chickadees chirring in the larch and looked at the country. Crystal lies just a few miles north of the Snake's watershed, but from here I could look down into the drainage of the river's northernmost tributary. I've always thought it bears the prettiest name of any stream in creation—the Little North Fork of the Clearwater. I could see some raw logging scars, new since my time, and familiar old blackened snags and mountain slopes of bright ceanothus brush, still-visible scars of the 1910 fire. Some of the mountainsides were blotched with brown. These were stands of larch, lovely, feathery-needled trees. All over the Snake River country they are under massive attack by an insect called the larch casebearer.

In my time the big disease in the forest had been blister rust. The rust, a fungus disease, attacks and kills the western white pine. White pine is tall, straight-trunked and symmetrical, and its easily worked wood has always been prized for the making of everything from match-sticks to house sidings to model airplanes. There are few men around who didn't spend a chunk of their childhood carving it with a single-edged razor blade.

Because of the high commercial value of white pine, foresters fought a battle against the blister rust for 40 years, but they lost. During part of its life cycle the rust lives on a shrub formally called ribes—the genus of wild gooseberries and currants that grow all through these mountains. In the 1930s the Forest Service started a campaign to ex-terminate ribes from the face of the earth, eliminate the rust and thus save the pine. When I was here in the '50s the woods were full of college boys who spent the summer slogging up and down the moun-tainsides, trying to poison or dig up and destroy every gooseberry and currant in creation. It was brutal work. A friend of mine, chasing a re-ported fire deep in the mountains, once spotted a young fellow vainly trying to climb up a steep brushy hillside. The youngster slipped again and again down to the bottom. Finally the boy threw down his Pulaski, raised his hands to the sky and yelled, "Up and down, up and down, up and down all day for a goddam dollar and a half an hour. Oh, Mom, get me out of this place!"

The blister-rust eradication program put a lot of young men of my generation through college, but it didn't halt the advance of the dis-ease. In the mid-1960s, three decades and some $80 million after it start-ed, the control program was abandoned. Though gooseberries and currants still grew throughout the mountains, most of the white pine had been killed.

Today, foresters are trying to re-establish the tree through devel-opment of a genetic strain that resists the disease. "In fact," says a For-est Service geneticist, "if we had known then what we know today, we might have been *planting* wild gooseberries during all those years, instead of destroying them.'' The more gooseberry bushes there were, he explained, the more the disease would have put pressure on the white pine to speed up the process of natural selection, and a resistant strain of pine would have emerged more quickly.

It would be unrealistic to suppose that experience with blister rust will cause us to abandon all traditional techniques of poisoning and uprooting when diseases strike the forest. But as with fire, there are clear signs of a new ecological sophistication, a new understanding of subtle biological inter-relationships. Because the forest managers now know the dangers to wildlife posed by pesticides, the insect that was attacking the larch that I could see from my seat on Crystal is going to be fought not with massive doses of insecticide, but with propagation of a parasitic wasp which specifically preys on this pest. No one knows whether the scheme will work. However, the fact that a biological rather than a chemical approach was being attempted is, in itself, a sign of healthy new thinking about the forest.

But some things never change. For all my newly acquired knowledge of fire and its role in the natural scene, sitting up there on Crystal I had a strong, atavistic desire to find and report a smoke. So toward the end of the long afternoon I went back up on the tower, took my binoculars and started to scan the country, ridge by ridge, draw by draw, looking for that soft gray wisp that starts a lookout's adrenaline flowing. To the north, nothing. To the east, there on Grandfather, what's that? No, it's just a little catface, a skinned-off slab of earth, a slide scar maybe. To the south—a plume there, something. But the color's wrong. Too yellow. Dust from a 'dozer, or a truck. To the west, hard against the sun, nothing. Nothing. I'd be lying if I said I wasn't disappointed.

NATURE WALK / A Climb to an Alpine Lake

PHOTOGRAPHS BY DAVID CAVAGNARO

Spring comes late, and quickly, to the peaks and alpine meadows of the northern Rocky Mountains. Not until June does the high country begin to brighten with the new season —and even then, deep remnants of the winter snowpack lie in ravines and shaded passes.

On a cool, late-June morning, hoping to catch the crest of the brief alpine spring, photographer David Cavagnaro and I started up the Iron Creek trail, about 50 miles northwest of Sun Valley. Our destination was Sawtooth Lake, a deep glacial tarn lying about five miles farther up the trail, under the shoulder of 10,190-foot Mount Regan.

The going was easy at first—a stroll along a winding track through flatland forest. Just past the point where the trail crossed Iron Creek, the country opened out into a grassy meadow. In the distance, the ragged peaks of the Sawtooth Range were washed with the golden light of early morning. The meadow before us was partially flooded—clearly, beavers had been at work: they had thrown a series of crude dams across the creek, and water from the spillways tumbled toward us in small, sparkling cascades.

The dams on the creek were only minor feats of beaver engineering. These powerful, diligent rodents have been known to build dams as much as 2,000 feet long, and they have felled trees five feet in diameter with their outsized incisors. In the course of their engineering, beavers sometimes do and sometimes do not build comfortable log lodges to live in. But they do seem to be obsessed with the desire to build *something*. When the 2,790-foot concrete and steel dam at Ice Harbor was being completed on the lower Snake, at one enormous lock gate a beaver turned up with a stick in his mouth. Apparently unfazed by the scope of the project, he was eager to assist his human colleagues.

We left the Iron Creek beavers' more modest monuments, and continued on. Some small birds, active in early morning, were chirping in the underbrush—juncos, perhaps, feeding on bugs and berries. Beside the trail, frost glistened on wild flowers—lacy meadow rue, wild strawberries and whorled penstemons. The penstemons are among the most common wild flowers of the Snake River country. Some 60 species grow hereabouts, in a variety of sizes and in every hue, from the palest pastels to a rich, saturated violet.

A FLOODED MEADOW ON IRON CREEK TRAIL

FROST-DAPPLED PENSTEMONS

The plant gets the name penstemon from the fact that the flower has a set of five stamens. Four of them produce pollen. The fifth, shaped like a little toothbrush, is sterile. When a bee visits the flower it is tickled on the belly by this stamen; as the bee wriggles in response, it rubs against the other stamens and coats its hair with pollen, which the bee then carries to the next flower.

As the morning grew warmer little butterflies called skippers and checkerspots danced like gleaming motes of dust in patches of sunlight. While I watched, a skipper with a

BUTTERFLIES ON VALERIAN BLOSSOMS   FALLEN LODGEPOLE PINES

one-inch wingspread and a checker-spot fully twice that size settled down to breakfast on the nectar of white valerian blossoms.

The Pioneering Lodgepole

The forest we walked through was made up mostly of lodgepole pine, one of the most common trees in the northern Rockies and easily identified by its twisted needles grouped in clusters of twos. The gentle hillsides above the trail were thick with these trees, and we passed one spot where dozens of fallen lodgepole trunks lay on the ground, interwoven like pick-up-sticks. Perhaps the trees had been killed by pinebark beetles or other insects. Relatively short-lived in this region, the lodgepoles become vulnerable to such infestation after a century or so.

Despite the trees' comparatively brief life span, lodgepole seeds germinate on even the most inhospitable soil, and the young trees have a vigorous early growth in the open places. Botanists call the tree a pioneer species and it is just that. Lodgepoles sprout on old burns, landslide scars and logged-over areas. They creep out into meadows and advance across sun-scorched sage flats, gradually infiltrating open land and turning it to forest.

Their trunks are very straight and slender and the wood, once seasoned, is light but tough. The Rocky Mountain Indians knew this and used the trees to support their tepees; hence the name lodgepole. The trees were so valued for this purpose that Plains tribes journeyed to the mountains to obtain them.

A YELLOW JACKET'S NEST

From one of the fallen logs hung a yellow jacket's papery, golfball-sized nest. These big, black-and-yellow wasps pack a powerful sting. The nest we saw was probably the home of a solitary queen, for only the queens live through the winter. This particular queen was now, no doubt, raising a brood of workers; these, along with later generations, would add to the size of the nest over the summer. Masticating wood and mixing the pulp with mouth secretion, they would manufacture a kind of paper to build successive layers onto the nest wall; by fall, the nest might reach the size of a football.

Not far beyond the yellow jacket's nest we found an anthill a yard across, covered with pine needles.

A PINE-NEEDLE ANTHILL

Mound-building ants, very common in the Idaho woods, lack the yellow jacket's powerful sting; nonetheless, they have a memorable bite and can be most aggressive when disturbed. We examined the nest with some care and moved on before any roving ant patrols discovered us.

Until now, the walking had continued to be easy. Though the vertical distance from the head of the trail to Sawtooth Lake is 2,200 feet, in the first mile and a half through the lodgepole forest, we had not gained more than a couple of hundred feet in altitude. But right ahead of us the land rose abruptly and our trail zigzagged upward, traversing the wall of the canyon above. It was late morning by now, and hot. Between the heat and the exertion of climbing, we began to sweat, and I was heartened to see ahead of us a clump of big Douglas fir.

The Douglas fir is one of my favorite trees. On the moist, humid coast of Washington, far to the northwest of Iron Creek, it grows to great size, trailing only the two species of Sequoia. One Douglas fir on the Olympic Peninsula measures more than 17 feet in diameter. In the drier Snake River country, they get nowhere near so big, of course. But they are stately trees even here, as much as three feet thick and 100 feet tall, with deeply furrowed russet bark several inches thick. Some of those near us swooped up from the ground in graceful curves; they had been bent when young saplings, possibly by snowbanks.

I am not the only admirer of the

Douglas fir. Pine squirrels are fond of them for their seeds. Often you can find squirrels' husking places beneath a stand of firs, with up to a bushel of shucked cones lying about. And since Douglas-fir wood is light in weight, straight grained and very strong, the trees are much sought by loggers. But to the hiker they have another kind of value—their feathery needles make a dense, cool shade, a welcome relief along the trail. They are, in fact, very good trees for sitting under, and that is what we did until we cooled off.

A Spider's Strategy

Refreshed, we started out again, slogging up the switchbacks. The pace was so slow that we got a close look at things along the trail. A checkered beetle had stopped to dine on the nectar of a yellow cinquefoil blossom. Nearby bloomed a cluster of bright yellow arnica, a source of a remedy used for sprains and bruises. On one of the petals a little crab spider lay in wait for some unsuspecting insect to wander by. The spider's color precisely matched that of the petal. So perfectly was the creature camouflaged that its chances of success looked good to me. These little hunters can change their hue to blend with whatever flower they happen to sit on. Had we put him on an Indian paintbrush he would have turned reddish.

Fat little puffballs popped up from the earth beside the trail. When young and still white-skinned, some of these spherical fungi can be quite good to eat, and some wild animals like them too. The older, yellow-

A SMALL GROVE OF DOUGLAS FIR

CHECKERED BEETLE ON CINQUEFOIL

PUFFBALLS BESIDE THE TRAIL

A CRAB SPIDER ON ARNICA

skinned puffballs like the ones we saw are not palatable.

Above the switchbacks the trail flattened out for a while, then swung back down along the upper stretches of Iron Creek. After crossing the stream on a log, we started climbing again. We were on the canyon's north-facing wall now, and it was much cooler here, for the trees grew more thickly on this wetter, shadier slope. We passed a lodgepole with a swatch of bark scaled off—the mark left by a hungry porcupine. The tree was dead, for the porky had ringed it right around, gnawing through the outer bark and destroying the phloem, or inner bark, which carries nutrients to and from the roots.

Porcupines have an even greater affinity for any wood that is flavored with salt or grease. When I was a fire-lookout years ago, a pair of porcupines used to keep me awake at night by gnawing on the back step of the cabin, and I had to bring the ax inside every night because porcupines regard a sweat-saturated tool handle as pure caviar.

LODGEPOLE GIRDLED BY PORCUPINES

Porkies are fairly common in the northern Rockies, where they grow into large, cumbersome creatures. Contrary to popular lore, they can't shoot their quills, but if any creature touches a porcupine, the barbed quills transfer themselves instantly from their owner to the offender.

For all this thorny protection, the porcupine is not completely secure from his enemies. Mountain lions, lynxes and other predators have learned the trick of flipping porkies over onto their backs by catching them on their noses—where there are few quills—and then attacking their unprotected bellies.

A Winsome Beggar

As we walked along, we occasionally caught a flicker of movement from small animals among the rocks. Sometimes it was a chipmunk, identifiable by the black stripes on his face as well as on his back. At other times we'd see a golden-mantled ground squirrel, which looks much like the chipmunk, but is larger and lacks the chipmunk's facial stripes. Both rodents are accomplished free-

AN INQUISITIVE CHIPMUNK

A GOLDEN-MANTLED GROUND SQUIRREL

SNOW-TOPPED PEAKS ABOVE ALPINE LAKE

loaders around campgrounds and on well-used trails, standing on their hind legs and begging winsomely.

The switchbacks finally came to an end. We reached a ridge and, looking down, we could see a cold, blue lake. According to our map it was Alpine Lake, and since it was now past lunchtime we descended a hundred feet or so to eat cheese and dried fruit on the lakeshore.

Alpine Lake is reputed to contain trout, but the only sign of life we saw was a spotted frog that floated in the shallows. I didn't envy him, for the lake was fed by melting snows and it was far too frigid for us to swim in. The northern Rockies do not offer a hospitable climate to thin-skinned and cold-blooded amphibians. The spotted frog is one of the few members of his genus that is adapted to this environment.

After lunch we began the steepest part of the climb: the trail rose almost 1,000 feet in a mile and a half. We were back on a southern exposure again, and we sweated hard on the open, sun-drenched slopes. Beds

A SPOTTED FROG BY THE LAKE SHORE

PURPLE PENSTEMONS AND YELLOW POTENTILLA ON A SOUTHERLY SLOPE ABOVE ALPINE LAKE

of penstemon and yellow pockets of potentilla grew along the trail. Potentilla is not a favorite on the menu of wild animals, but they will turn to it when such preferred plants as the ceanothus—both the red-stemmed and the sticky laurel—have been overgrazed. It is thus a kind of litmus test for wildlife managers—if potentilla has been heavily grazed, the range is overcrowded.

Here and there appeared the red twinberry with its pairs of trumpet-shaped flowers. The plant gets its name from the juicy berries, which are joined to one another by twos, like Siamese twins. Generically, the twinberry is a honeysuckle, one that grows not as a vine but as an upright shrub. The blossoms of the bushes we passed had a lovely fragrance, and later in the year the ripe berries would make an attractive dessert for foraging black bears, grizzlies or grouse.

A BOULDER IN A SNARE OF ROOTS

Siberian wallflower sprouted out from the rock faces beside the trail. Like many of the other flowers along Iron Creek trail, this member of the mustard family climbs up the mountainsides as the season advances, following the retreating snows. In May we would have found it blooming lower down—a couple of weeks from now it would be blossoming 1,000 feet above, on the slopes around Sawtooth Lake. Chipmunks and other alpine rodents nibble its leaves at the lower levels; higher up it is forage for elk, deer and goats.

Wind-Warped Trees

As we climbed, the country grew more rugged. Up here, the trees—alpine firs and limber and whitebark pines—had been stunted and shaped by wind and the weight of the snow. Some had been uprooted by the wind; we found one wind-thrown tree that had a two-foot boulder clutched in its upthrust roots. Underfoot the ground was marshy from the snowmelt, and random patches of snow lay across the trail. Soft now in the warmth of afternoon, the snow would firm up overnight and be almost as hard as ice by morning.

After what seemed like a very long

TRUMPETS OF TWINBERRY

SIBERIAN WALLFLOWERS

A BED OF LINANTHASTRUM

INDIAN PIPES RISING THROUGH SNOW

LARVAL CASES OF CADDISFLIES

stretch, the trail emerged into a clearing carpeted with lush grass and flowers. A hummock of white linanthastrum, looking like miniature phlox, grew at our feet. Blossoms of Indian pipe burst up through a patch of unmelted snow. The latter plant, named for its pipe-bowl-shaped flower, is a parasite. The roots take nourishment from fungi that grow on dead leaves and other plant litter. (Indians used the pipe's juices as a soothing eye lotion.)

The meadow was very wet, crisscrossed with little streams, and at the head of the meadow lay a small pond. The water was still, with little sign of life, but along the shore we found a pair of empty caddisfly cases. The trout fisherman in me stirred with anticipation. These cases, of sand grains stuck together with salivary secretions, are the shells in which the caddisfly spend the larval stage. The delicate-winged adults are a staple in the trout diet.

Already planning my strategy for evening fishing, I walked to the head of the meadow, crossed through a band of whitebark pines and came out on the shore of Sawtooth Lake. Surrounded by snow, still partly covered with melted ice, the lake was dark blue, shading away to black toward its deep center. Just across the lake stood the summit block of Mount Regan, the late sun glinting on its flanks. The scene was beautiful, but with that cold, unforgiving look of the high mountains—a look that made me feel, as we began to make camp, that I was here only on nature's sufferance.

TRAIL'S END VISTA OF SAWTOOTH LAKE AND MOUNT REGAN

4/ River Time

The water runs with great violence from one rock to the other on each side foaming & roreing thro rocks in every direction, So as to render the passage of any thing impossible. WILLIAM CLARK/ *JOURNALS*

After we finished loading the rafts we stood on the bank of the Salmon River in a fine mist of rain. I hitched up the edge of my poncho to check my wrist watch and remembered that I had left the watch behind for fear that it would get thoroughly soaked. For the next 10 days, I would have no idea of the time. I mentioned this to Boyd Norton, the photographer, and he laughed. "No matter," he said. "From now on, there's nothing but river time."

South of the Selway-Bitterroot lie the Idaho Primitive Area and the adjoining Salmon River Breaks Primitive Area. This is the country drained by the Snake's mighty tributary, the Salmon, the stream long known as the River of No Return, because a voyage on it was a one-way trip: down. Until the recent advent of the jet boat, which can blast upstream through heavy rapids, the Salmon always lived up to its nickname. One late-19th Century freight shipper used to run supplies downriver and, at the end of each trip, sell his boat for firewood.

The Salmon and its major tributaries, particularly the Middle Fork, are at the center of the Snake River country's plexus of white-water rivers—including the South Fork, the Selway and the Bruneau. Perfect for river running, their waters are clean and mostly crystal clear, and the wilderness they flow through is as pristine as any in the nation. If, for example, you were to put your raft or kayak into the water at Dagger Falls on the Middle Fork and start downstream, you could follow the river for 100 miles to its confluence with the surging main Salmon. Then you could float the Salmon for another 100 miles before reaching the first significant human community, the little logging town of Riggins, Idaho. Thus it is possible to travel, as I did, some 200 miles of long, swift runs and frothing rapids, almost all in total wilderness.

The Middle Fork of the Salmon is a delightful small river that drops steeply and has slam-bang rapids around every other bend. It flows through dark coniferous forests and spectacular gorges, and except for a couple of fly-in lodges on pockets of privately owned land, it traverses country that shows no sign of man. I went down the river with the Forest Service patrol—two men in kayaks, the rest of us in two big sweep boats with five days' supplies. We left from the base of Dagger Falls on an afternoon in late June; Dick Estes, a tall, soft-spoken ranger who bears an astonishing resemblance to Fred MacMurray, stood in the middle of our rubber raft, manning the sweeps.

As we pushed off from the bank, the current swung the raft's broad bow, and then the river took us. The banks were steep and dense with fir and spruce. We drifted between them at the speed of the current, or a touch slower perhaps, like a chip of wood on the water. This speed is the joy of a trip by raft—neither too fast nor too slow. You have a sensation of being one with the river. And though the water on which you move may sometimes be dangerous, the raft is simultaneously a part of the water and a refuge from it.

A real river runner never says "raft," as I do. The professional, aware of important technical considerations, speaks rather of Yampas and Greens and Salmon River boats, sweep boats and ten-mans, Hatch rigs, and the big air-filled pontoons called bloatos or baloneys. He will have nothing whatever to do with those familiar yellow survival rafts, which invariably get torn to pieces in the rapids and which he speaks of disdainfully as rubber duckies. Then there are kayaks, C-1 canoes (which, to you and me, are indistinguishable from kayaks) and wooden Mackenzie River dories with their pointed ends.

Most of these craft are controlled by standard paddles or paired oars. But a sweep boat works differently from all the others. It has two enormous paddle-like appendages, mounted not on the sides like oars, but off the bow and stern. Dick Estes stood erect on a platform in the middle of the raft, holding the sweep handles chest high, and more or less rowed with them, steering the raft sideways back and forth across the river. Approaching two big rocks, Dick maneuvered the boat so as to enter exactly the piece of current flowing through the gap.

Getting safely into the gaps is mainly a matter of anticipation. The boatman must be experienced enough to read the water with great accuracy. Otherwise he may put himself in the wrong piece of river, and there is no going back for another try. But if he reads the water well, like Dick, he finds his pieces of current with a minimum of effort, and lets the river do the rest of the work.

For the less experienced it isn't so easy. Only a mile or so downstream from where we started, we found a rubber ducky wrapped around a rock; and a little later we saw a second one flattened and abandoned on the riverbank. Farther on we came upon a party, knee-deep in the rushing current, trying to horse a raft off a rocky riffle where it had lodged. Later, below a modest rapids, Dick pulled our sweep boat in to the bank—he wanted to wait and see how the other people would make out. Pretty soon the raft appeared upstream, four men paddling like crazy but without any coordination. By the time they got into the first of the white water they were paddling even faster, in opposite directions; halfway through, the raft started spinning like a top, caroming off rocks. A moment later the river spat the boat out, backward but miraculously upright, into the quiet pool below the rapids.

Dick shook his head. "They'll be walking out," he said. "They'll never make it through the worst rapids handling a boat that way. We try to discourage people like that from running the river, but we don't think we have the right to stop them if they're determined to do it. If they do make it, they'll never forget the adventure."

More than 4,000 people run the Middle Fork each year. Use of the river increased so rapidly in the early '70s that the Forest Service had to institute a strict reservation system. But the Middle Fork remains a difficult and dangerous river. On one recent July weekend, 165 people were involved in one mishap or another, and 13 boats were wrecked. But virtually all well-led expeditions get through safely, with a fair measure of excitement but no real trouble. In 1972 the Las Vegas gambler Amarillo Slim wangled a bet with a man—one apparently ignorant of the number of people running the Middle Fork—who wagered that Slim couldn't make it. Slim hired a professional guide, ran the river without serious incident and collected $31,000. Estes laughed, "I wish somebody would make me that bet."

Boyd Norton had been right about that strange tempo he called river time. After two or three days on the water I began to feel that life had a new and pleasant measure. If you are backpacking, you always have an

Massive slopes of snow-dusted granite flank the Middle Fork where it emerges from the Idaho Primitive Area to join the Salmon River.

acute sense of time and position, for each foot of ground is hard won: three more miles, 1,200 feet to climb, then the bad switchbacks over the divide and now it's half past three, Mountain Daylight. Getting late. But on the river, hours and days merge and blend—the meter stops running. Just how long ago was it that we camped by the hot spring? And is today Tuesday, Wednesday or Thursday? Does anybody know what time it is? Does anybody really care?

As we floated on down, the river was always changing yet somehow always the same. The steep-walled, timbered canyon opened out to sage-covered hills, then closed in again so that our boats seemed pinched between 1,000-foot walls. The river ran bright and sunlit through the riffles, slipped into long, deep black pools where we drifted lazily, soaking up the sun and casting flies to the little cutthroat trout that rose from the dark water. Then from the rapids ahead came the sound that tensed the guts.

Except for deceptive Velvet Falls, which is anything but soft and smooth, most of the rapids on the Middle Fork have names that are guaranteed to put a chill on the blood: Powerhouse, Artillery, Pistol Creek. The main Salmon offers many others—Gunbarrel, Devil's Teeth, Split Rock, Growler and Dried Meat.

At each rapids Dick Estes braced himself, deftly positioned the big raft with quick strokes of his sweeps and down we dropped through the roiling water, the raft rearing and bucking, the spray soaking us through. At a very small rapids Dick let me try the sweeps, and I was astonished at the river's force, transmitted to me by the big paddles. The sweeps seemed alive, uncontrollable. The handles shoved me backward, almost knocking me over. My timing hopelessly off, I drove the sweeps forward, but the river fell away ahead and the bow sweep missed the water entirely. We slewed around and sideswiped a rock, but the raft simply bounced on through and we reached the pool below safely—through no fault of mine.

River time. At dusk the Vaux's swifts and violet-green swallows cut their intricate traceries against the canyon walls; at night the campfire and the stories and the smoky taste of bourbon. One night, long after dark, I made my way back through the forest away from the river to a hot spring in a little meadow. I shucked my clothes and squatted there, shoulder deep in the warm flow. It was eerie. The night was totally black. The water had a strong smell of sulfur, and little bubbles of gas seeping from the ooze on the bottom scurried up my back like tiny mice. A sudden sound, a great snorting noise from right next to me—I scrabbled for my flashlight and switched it on full in the face of a huge mule-deer buck that stood only a few feet away. He snorted again, as terrified as I, then exploded away into the dark. Later, when I shone the flashlight in a slow circle, I saw his eyes, iridescent points of pink, glowing like coals, as he stood far back in dark woods and watched me.

One day on the river we stopped at a deep hole to fish for salmon. The Salmon River, including the Middle Fork, was named by early settlers in recognition of its great run of these fish. Known here as Chinook and on the Pacific Coast as king salmon, the species that dominates this river is the largest of all the salmon family, and each year hundreds of thousands come up from the ocean to spawn.

Angling for Chinook is a popular sport through much of the Snake River country, though actually catching one, it seemed to me, was something like hooking a big striper out of the surf—sort of a special dispensation from God. Thousands apply, but few are chosen.

We climbed a little cliff about 20 feet above the water and rigged up our outfits, baiting the hooks with stinking clusters of salmon eggs. During their 800-mile journey from the ocean to the headwaters of the Salmon, the fish do not eat at all, but sometimes they can be induced to strike at clusters of eggs or big bright lures. Why they do so is a mystery. Some say that the fish are annoyed by the bright objects and attack out of sheer ill temper. Others say that they crush and destroy anything that even resembles salmon eggs because they instinctively want to eliminate competition for their own spawn. Until someone is able to psychoanalyze a fish, there is no way of knowing.

We stood on the clifftop and cast our bait toward the head of the green pool below us. Then we retrieved very, very slowly, for the pool was perhaps 30 feet deep, and the bait must bump right along the rocky bottom where the fish lie.

Complete the retrieve, cast again. Again. For someone who likes to chase trout around with a flyrod, this is a slow and boring kind of fishing. I found it hard to concentrate. I paid more attention to the country than to the fishing, looking at the big stands of ponderosa along the river, and at the overcast that was slowly covering the sky. Fishing close to the bottom in this way, I got hung up on the rocks a lot, cussed, struggled with the line, finally broke a leader and lost my terminal tackle. We all did that. We sweated in spite of the overcast, crouched over our outfits, tying on new hooks and leaders and noisome gobs of eggs.

An hour or so and I was ready to give in. One more cast. Every fisherman always does. It's the last one, do it right, the slow retrieve, feel it hit bottom. That's that. And damn, hung up again on a rock.

Angry, I jerked my rod. The rod jerked back—hard.

"I've got one!" I yelled. I couldn't believe it. The rod was bent in a sharp parabola, throbbing in a solid way that I could feel right down to my heels. In a second Dick Estes was there beside me. "You sure have got one. Easy, easy, don't horse him."

There was enormous pressure on the rod. I looked at my reel and saw to my horror that the line wasn't running out and knew that my leader couldn't take that kind of tension. Stupid! Last time I'd got hung up on the rocks I had cinched the drag down tight to break off and then forgot to ease off. As quickly as I could, I slacked the drag a little and the fish started taking line. No spectacular run, he was going to beat me with brute strength. He just went deep and dogged it, shaking his head so I could feel him through my bones.

"You better try to work him upstream," Dick said. "If that fish ever starts downstream he'll strip your line and keep right on going; you won't have a chance."

"Work him upstream? I can't even move him." I didn't work him anyplace; we just stayed there locked in our tug of war. Finally the tension eased. He was coming up and then I saw him for the first time, a lightness rising from the black water, growing, broadening. Near the surface he rolled, and he looked to me the size of a submarine.

I thought: there is no way that I will ever be able to land this fish. Then, with a twist of his broad tail he took back the line he had given me and disappeared into the dark water again. Now he began his runs, powerful surges, but he erred here. He did not run downstream, which would have defeated me, but upstream, fighting the current as well as the pressure of the rod. I gained on him. My arms were getting stiff but he was tiring too.

The salmon came up again, close in. When he rolled I could see the fierce-looking, sharply hooked nose, like an eagle's beak, that signifies the male. His eye, sunken deep behind a ridge of flesh, was malevolent as a boar's. We were eye to eye for that moment, and then he dived again with a surge that would have pulled me into the pool if Dick hadn't been holding my collar.

The dive was the salmon's final gesture. On a grassy bank at the edge of the cliff we beached and killed him. He was 40 inches long and so heavy I couldn't hold him up for a picture. I'd beaten him.

I guess.

A bright-eyed golden marmot, the watchman of the high country, stands ready to whistle his shrill warning against any predators that may be about. The marmot's tour of sentry duty lasts only through the three to four warm months of spring and summer; he hibernates the remainder of the year in his rocky burrow.

"Though boys throw stones at frogs in sport," said the Greek poet Bion, "the frogs do not die in sport but in earnest."

The life cycle of the Pacific salmon is one of the most magical and mysterious phenomena in the whole spectrum of nature. The Chinook that I killed was nearing the end of an incredible journey that had begun five or six years before in a tiny headwater stream of the Salmon River. After hatching, baby salmon spend some months in fresh water, then begin to drift slowly downstream, tail first, until they reach the Pacific Ocean. There they strike out for blue water. In schools of hundreds of thousands, so densely packed that a fish cannot turn without striking against its neighbor, the salmon range up the coast of British Columbia and the Alaska Peninsula. Some follow the food-rich Arctic waters out along the Aleutian Islands almost to Japan before they circle back toward home. In the salt water, the salmon grow with astonishing speed, and Chinooks have been known to reach a weight of more than 100 pounds.

At the age of anywhere from three to six years the fish return to the mouth of the Columbia and begin their 800-mile, two-month struggle up the Columbia, up the Snake, up the Salmon, toward the very tributary where they were born. This homing instinct is so powerful that the fish will jump over high waterfalls and climb fish ladders built around dams to reach their home stream. And the instinct is incredibly accurate. Again and again in their journey the salmon have to choose which fork in the river to take; yet in experiments with tagged fish, they have almost always found their way to their birthplace stream.

Ichthyologists theorize that salmon accomplish this feat of navigation through their extremely acute sense of smell. Each birthplace stream has a precise and individual chemical composition, which conveys a unique scent. In all the years at sea, the salmon rarely forgets the smell of home waters, and each traces this tenuous thread all the way from the Pacific.

In order to reach their spawning beds today, the fish face almost insuperable obstacles created by man. On the downstream voyage perhaps 10 per cent of the young fish are killed or injured going through the turbines of each major dam. Others lose their way in the slack water of reservoirs and never reach the sea. In all, probably fewer than 40 per cent of the young fish ever reach salt water. Commercial fishermen take an enormous toll of the maturing fish—indeed, Pacific salmon make up the most valuable commercial fishery in the world.

When the adults start back up the Columbia to spawn, their passage is made much more difficult by man's manipulation of the river. First, the salmon must ascend the steep fish ladders built around each dam. Once the salmon enter fresh water they fast, and must live on reserves of body fat, absorbing half their weight in the course of the trip. Any extra exertion diminishes the chances of reaching the spawning beds.

Today a salmon must pass eight dams on the Columbia and lower Snake to reach the nursery streams of central Idaho, and each dam presents an insidious danger. As the water crashes over the dam spillways it imprisons large quantities of air. The water in the pools below the dam becomes supersaturated with nitrogen from the air, and salmon resting deep in the pools pick up this nitrogen in the course of breathing. When they rise to the surface to continue their upstream journey, nitrogen bubbles form in their bloodstream and the fish become afflicted with nitrogen narcosis—the crippling, sometimes lethal, sickness that divers know as the bends. The salmon's skin blisters and ulcerates, blood vessels burst in its eyes, and even if the fish does survive, it may be blind. In a bad year, a large percentage of the entire salmon run may be wiped out by the bends.

When the fish finally reach the shallow streams where they were born, the females begin beating with their tails to form a spawning bed called a redd. (When I was a small child, my elderly grandmother used to talk about "redding up the living room," by which she meant cleaning the place. It wasn't until I began to learn about the salmon that I realized the common origin of the words.) The males, meanwhile, square off to fight for the honor of breeding with the females.

As the salmon prepare to mate, they are already beginning to die. The males are battered and torn from combat, the females are weakened from the labor of building the redd, all are exhausted from their 800-mile journey. But they still must consummate the act for which they have come so far. Side by side on the redd, touching each other, vibrating their bodies, they work toward a moment of climax when they expel eggs and sperm in a great gasping release.

The running water mixes sperm and eggs together; the two fish expand the redd, and for a few days they continue to mate. But soon they are spent. The weakened male starts to drift downstream. The female attempts to stay with the redd to prevent other fish from disturbing the eggs, but soon she weakens too. And now, within a few days of mating, both males and females will die. Not some of them—as with other sea-

A herd of bighorn sheep browses during a February snow flurry near the confluence of the Middle Fork and the Salmon rivers. In winter, the ram, distinguished by his heavy, spiral horns, stands guard over the harem of ewes that he has collected during the fall mating season. After the lambs are born in the spring, he joins a bachelor band for the summer, leaving the care of the young to the ewes.

Masses of black lava, congealed some 100,000 years ago, form cliffs above the Owyhee.

The afternoon sun glows on a canyon wall

made of brown sandstone and a golden volcanic rock known as tuff. At lower right stands the crumbling remnant of a basalt ledge.

Like the columns and spires of an Asian temple, chiseled rocks of volcanic tuff line the side of the Owyhee Canyon. These remarkably

sculpted land formations develop as rainfall slowly erodes and enlarges the vertical fractures in the once-smooth surface of the rock.

5/ "Rocky Mountain High"

The land stands up unrefined,
Roughhewn by whittling winds.
Its trees stream away like clippership sails
Tacking the northerlies before a swelling gale.

R. J. PETRILLO/ *BANJO PICKER WIND*

We left the grassy meadows at the foot of the waterfall on Toxaway Lake at about 9:30 in the morning and started climbing toward the Snowyside divide. We were halfway along on a week's backpacking trip and the dozen of us had divided into two groups. At about 7:30, Dawn Patrol had marched out of camp with the forward-tilting, purposeful stride of dedicated hikers, as Sloths and Sluggards were just emerging from their sleeping bags. A couple of hours later, after several cups of coffee and some groaning, we Sloths hit the trail.

The July morning was cool and sunny, with dew on the grass, the sound of the waterfall loud on the ears; and the abrupt mountains, standing sharp as canines, were crisp and yellow-pink in the morning light. Our route led into the Sawtooth Range, north of Sun Valley. Except for the Tetons these are the most stunning mountains of the Snake River country, and thus among the most beautiful peaks on the continent. (In case you are wondering—like the man who wrote the pet shop and said, "Send me one mongoose, and while you're at it, send me another"—the plural of Sawtooth is Sawtooths.)

The Sawtooths are a backpacker's range. The trails are well maintained and, unlike the Selway-Bitterroot, where distances are great, the topography is compact, as if designed on a human scale. A loop trip of 30 miles can take you to a dozen high-country lakes, over several passes and into a variety of river drainages, with new hunks of mountain scenery revealing themselves, like the successive sets of a play, every time you cross a ridge.

As usual with me, on this morning the first half mile was agony. Coming up out of the meadows and into the spruce-fir forest I felt pains like hot wires being drawn up the back of my calves, and my breath came short and heavy. My nose ran with exertion; sweat trickled down my forehead and misted my sunglasses.

The beginning of a long hike is always the worst. For me it is a stumbling search for the right pace, that rate at which you can cover the most ground with the least effort. Very fit people put packs on their backs and stride up a mountain as if walking to the corner for a quart of milk. The rest of us plod, one short step after another. A brisk hiking pace is about four miles per hour—but not with a pack and not in the mountains. The backpacker's rule of thumb is half an hour per mile, plus half an hour for every 1,000 feet of elevation gained, not counting rest stops. And I am usually slower than that. In steep country and carrying a pack, seven or eight miles make for a full, hard day.

And so I plodded. I couldn't see much. The tent, high on the pack behind my neck, made it difficult to tilt my head back to look at the scenery. My head was bowed, my field of vision restricted: a band of brilliant purple penstemon along the trail, a scarlet dab of Indian paintbrush. Mica flakes glittered in the trail dust, which was imprinted with a pattern of little crosses—the sign of the Vibram-soled climbing boots of Dawn Patrol, two hours ahead. The handle of the ice ax I carried as a walking stick made dots among the crosses.

A telltale squiggle seen earlier on a map, snaking back and forth across tightly bunched contour lines, had forecast when the real pain would begin: where the trail began to switchback a little way beyond the lake. The switchbacks, crisscrossing the face of the steep mountainside, made the ascent possible, but barely.

As we trudged up out of the timber into the more open country above, I felt the hot wire on my calves again and my breath came short. Slow down now, I thought. Shorten the pace to little chop steps. A rock in the trail—don't step up on it; that one high lift of the leg will use up the energy of a dozen steps. Walk around it. Now step, lock the leg, pause and rest; step, lock the leg, pause.

Slowly, slowly the country fell away behind us. Must pain be a part of the wilderness experience? I wondered. For people in better shape than I, this trail would involve little pain, but then, they would push themselves harder and farther until they pressed against their own limits. I began to ask myself why we didn't simply sit under a tree somewhere and watch the grass grow and hear the birds sing? What the devil are we doing here, climbing this impossible mountainside and humping these packs we've learned to hate? If we want to look at the pretty scenery, why not go to the Alps and ride the cable cars?

Well, I'd learned that my thoughts always ran that way when I was climbing a mountain, and I'd also learned that when I got to the top all those thoughts would go away.

This time the top came suddenly; around one last switchback and there we were in the pass. I stuck my ice ax point-down in a little snowbank and leaned on it, breathing hard. We stood at 9,200 feet. The pink granite summit of Snowyside loomed another 1,459 feet above us to the west, then swept away in a long arcing ridge of sheer pinnacles that swung south, then east to the towering wall of El Capitán. The wind blew high and cold. It sucked the sweat from my body, blew gray scud across distant ranges that looked like the winter side of hell. The wind carried a clean, sharp smell of snow and cold granite. Far off to the east, beyond the mouth of the canyon and across the valley, the rolling summits of the White Cloud Peaks gleamed cream-white in the sun.

From the pass I looked across a mountain architecture that verged on the melodramatic—a terrain of sudden peaks and knife-edged ridges and sheer faces. High, cold, windswept, this is not an easy country for living things, and the plants and animals that can survive here are those that can tolerate hard times.

The mountains surrounding me were the product of a geological cataclysm. Sixty to 100 million years ago, great bodies of rock deep within the earth were heated to the melting point by internal pressure and began to work their way upward. Cooling as they rose, the molten bodies ultimately lifted above the level of the earth's surface, where erosion removed the overlying rocks. Today they stand as one of the more massive bodies of granitic rock on the face of the earth, stretching about 250 miles from the Sawtooths through range after range of the Idaho mountains all the way north to the Clearwater River.

Later this mass of rock was reshaped and sculpted by the glaciers of the Pleistocene epoch. These frozen rivers, formed high in the mountains where the lower layers of snow were converted by pressure into ice, gravitated slowly down the mountainsides like an extremely thick syrup. They gouged away at the high slopes where they had been born, eating bowl-shaped basins out of the rock, great scoops in the mountaintops I could see from the pass. Carrying loads of rock debris, the glaciers then plowed through stream valleys lower down, cutting them wider, changing them from V-shaped, water-cut channels to broad, U-shaped canyons. Finally reaching the warmer temperatures of the valley floor, the glaciers melted back, dumping their loads of rock and gravel.

Today, in the Sawtooths or the White Clouds or the Tetons, the countryside is a display case of classic glacial patterns. As you approach almost any valley leading into the mountains—such as the one behind Pettit Lake in the Sawtooths—the sagebrush desert ends in a height of land that may be anywhere from a few feet to several hundred feet above the level of the plain. This piece of elevated terrain is the moraine, a natural depository of rocky debris left here when warmer weather put an end to the glacier's massive bulldozing. (Big moraines can be very disheartening geological features for a backpacker. Returning bone-tired from a trip, you get down to the foot of the mountains —only to find yourself faced with the prospect, in the very last mile, of climbing over a 500-foot moraine to reach the roadhead.)

A typical moraine forms a natural dam at the mouth of the valley, so that on the side of a moraine toward the mountain there is nearly always a lake. These moraine-dammed lakes must be the foreground feature of half the color pictures made by amateur photographers traveling in the Snake River country. Deep and blue, bordered by pine forests and with the high peaks rising abruptly from their far shores, they are, without exception, postcard-pretty.

If you proceed around the lake and go farther up into the canyon behind it you will find a broad meadow or a forest with near-vertical walls on each side; again, the classic pattern of glacial carving. At the head of the canyon, thousands of feet above the original valley, you will reach an amphitheater carved from the mountain peak. This is the cirque, the birthplace of the original glacier. Here again, you will likely find a lake, lying in the hollow eaten out by the ice. These cirque lakes are, if anything, even more beautiful than the morainal lakes in the valleys—deep blue bowls surrounded by lush alpine meadows and summer collars of snow, with the high peaks reflected in the water.

Of the glaciers that shaped these mountains, only a few vestigial miniglaciers remain in the Tetons. But the chiseling and sculpting of the mountains still goes on. At night in a high-country camp, you can hear it. Suddenly you will come stark, staring awake in your sleeping bag to the roar of a rockfall from the mountain faces above. Water has frozen in the cracks of the granite, pried off some great slab and sent it falling out into space. And as the rock thunders down, echoing and reverberating, it sounds as if the whole mountain is falling. Afterward you will lie in your sleeping bag for a long time before going back to some kind of fitful dozing.

The snow—though no longer of glacial depth—remains a force that determines the nature of the country. This land is steep and arid, with only a sprinkling of summer rain, most of which quickly runs downhill and is gone. If it were not for the snowpack, born in the blizzards of winter to release a vital ration of meltwater, life in the mountains and in the valleys below would hardly be possible at all.

The snowpack is a source of wonder and bemusement to visitors all through the northern Rockies. Stop at any high mountain pass on, say, the Fourth of July weekend, and the out-of-state cars will be parked along the snowdrifts, the kids throwing snowballs and having a fine time, the adults wondering just how it can be, in the middle of summer, on a day when the temperature is pushing 90°F. that 12 feet of snow lies along the side of the road. Here at the pass below Snowyside, a piece of the snowpack was holding out where my ice ax rested.

The pack does not melt—at least not quickly—for several reasons. First, snow is one of the most efficient natural insulating materials, a principle Eskimos have always understood. In their igloos, they can sleep naked. Second, the quantity of heat needed to melt ice or snow is enormous. The same amount of heat required to melt a gram of snow will raise the temperature of a gram of water from 32°F. to 176°F.

Snow is such an efficient reflector that most of the sun's rays simply bounce off the surface without appreciable effect. Inside the pack, regardless of the outside air temperature, the temperature among the frozen crystals can never be more than 32°F.; thus the water that does melt on the surface is likely to refreeze as it percolates down through the pack. Even rain may have no effect, often freezing as it penetrates and reinforcing the existing snow.

In this fashion, rather than diminishing, the snowpack lasts in the mountains for months, often around the year from snowfall to snowfall, distributing its life-giving water supply gradually throughout the whole summer. That is why high-country meadows, like the ones I saw below the pass at Snowyside, are lush and green. Moreover, the amount of runoff from the snowpack is highly predictable. By measuring the average depth of the snowpack, the flow of the rivers in the Snake River

Little Boulder Creek, a trout-filled tributary

the Salmon River, meanders lazily through meadows beneath a dark stand of alpine firs and the granite spires of the White Cloud Peaks.

country can usually be forecast with precision throughout the year. A river runner can get a prediction for spring and summer water conditions on an undammed stream months ahead of time. Even the progress of the salmon run, which is directly affected by the rivers' water volume, can be estimated by measuring the pack.

The mountain snowpack has other consequences, not always so benign, as we learned while climbing up from Toxaway Lake. Early in the morning we had passed through an area of devastation. The steep slope rising to the right of the trail was bare of everything but grasses and small shrubs. Below to the left lay a jumble of ravaged trees, piled like jackstraws, their roots sticking into the air. The wreckage represented the aftermath of a snow avalanche.

Avalanches are commonplace in this country of precipitous mountains and deep snow. Starting from a cornice or a high ravine, they can rip down a mountainside at 200 miles per hour, compressing the air ahead of the thundering snow into a deadly blast that crushes everything in its path. Only the fact that few people are in the mountains in the winter prevents avalanches from causing regular front-page tragedies. Back during the gold rush, when many more people wintered in the northwestern mountains, avalanches did cause frequent disasters, wiping out entire mining camps. In recent decades, Western ski resorts have tried to control the perils of snowslides by closing off dangerous areas or deliberately starting avalanches with explosive charges on steep slopes before the ski runs are opened.

Generally these avalanche programs have been successful, though each year in the United States perhaps half a dozen skiers are killed or seriously injured by snowslides. Out in the natural wilderness, however, away from humans, the avalanches probably do more good than harm. Despite the devastation in their wakes, they open up forested slopes and create brush fields that are good browse for deer and elk.

Sun and wind also have a fundamental effect on the life and the look of these mountains. Stand on the west side of the broad basin below the Sawtooths; turn toward the east, and you can see their influence. The southern slopes are relatively bare—the home of sagebrush and bitterbrush and other plants of the arid lands. The northern slopes are covered with trees, protected from the full force of the summer sun and the desiccating southwesterly winds that prevail.

Over in the Tetons, Blacktail Butte in the middle of Jackson Hole is a textbook example of these effects. Seen from the south it is a bald, treeless hill; from the north it is a heavily forested mountain; from the west it is two-toned—pine green on its northern slopes, sage gray on its southern slopes, with the line between drawn sharp, as if scribed with a ruler. Here, going from the desert to the forest is only a matter of crossing a narrow ridge.

After we dropped down the far side of Snowyside pass, we camped at a glacial tarn called Alice Lake. Once we were settled, I sat in front of my tent and scanned the granite faces above with my binoculars, hoping to spot a mountain goat and be entertained by its cliffside acrobatics. I found dozens of false goats—little goat-sized pockets of unmelted snow—but never the real thing. I am unlucky in goats, having seen only a handful in my lifetime. But so are most people, for goats are the natural residents of only three of the contiguous United States—Idaho, Washington and Montana. They are common nowhere and they live in the most difficult country inhabited by any large land mammal. Their forbidding habitat in the high mountains is beset by violent storms and gale-force winds and bone-cracking cold all winter, and sometimes during the summer as well. Anything that lives in this high country seems to defy not only gravity but common sense, and the goats are able to do so only because of their extraordinary physical adaptations.

The mountain goat is not a goat at all, but a relative of the chamois, an Old World antelope. It does have one thing in common with its domestic namesake, though—a gourmand's appetite. The goat will eat anything from mosses to tree bark, as indeed it must in order to survive in its austere world. The animal's survival is further abetted by the exceptionally warm and heavy overcoat it wears, a coat of genuine wool so dense and fine as to be considered superior to cashmere. And the goat is a truly astonishing climber, able to negotiate steep rock faces that would intimidate a circus aerialist. Its hooves are specially engineered—hard-edged but with rubbery pads on the bottom—so that the animal can maintain footing on its precarious highways. But goats, like high-wire artists, operate close to their margin of safety. On rare occasions they may misjudge their capabilities and fall to their death on the rocks below.

With its shaggy white coat and shoe-button eyes, the goat reminds me of a stuffed toy, apparently as friendly and cuddly as a teddy bear. But the look is deceptive, for the goats are animals of extreme choler. Although they often travel together in small bands, they appear to detest one another's company. All adult goats are surrounded by an invisible barrier that some biologists call a "zone of intolerance." This zone has a radius varying from a few feet to several yards, depending on circumstances and the goat's sourness of mood. Any animal that steps inside the zone is likely to get a sharp thrust from a black horn. And the mountain goat's horns, though small, are very sharp and serious weapons. The renowned turn-of-the-century naturalist Ernest Thompson Seton called the goat's horns "two terrible little black bayonets," and wrote of one goat that fought and killed 13 dogs before being shot, and of another that killed a grizzly bear.

When two billies fight they don't butt heads like sheep, but try to thrust the points of their horns into each other's flanks. Goats are quite capable of killing each other in combat, and Seton tells of a billy that disemboweled a rival with a horn thrust. And for all the bellicosity of the male, the nanny seems to be even more touchy and aggressive. Given the nanny's more-or-less chronic ill temper, the billy approaches the act of love as does the porcupine—very carefully. He grovels, does little courtship dances and doesn't try to invade her zone of intolerance until he feels sure that he will be received with ardor rather than a quick shot in the brisket.

Considering their apparent distaste for each other, it is rather a wonder that goats procreate at all. While I'm sure that any biologist would laugh at the suggestion, I can't help speculating that their curmudgeonly behavior could in itself be an adaptation to their severe environment—a means of controlling their population through mutual dislike.

Population control is something of a necessity in high alpine country, which is not capable of supporting animal life in large numbers or in much variety. Aside from the goats you may see a marmot or the furry little pika, both occasionally found at timberline and above where there seems virtually no food at all—but where predators are also scarce. At these altitudes there are not even many birds. Once in a while you may hear a raucous chirring sound from the stunted trees and glimpse the flickering black and white wings of the Clark's nutcracker, a big seed-eating bird related to the jay.

People often call these birds camp robbers, perhaps confusing them with the smaller Canada jays that live lower down in the same country—brazen customers that hang around a campground demanding alms. Sometimes they will take food right from your hand or your plate. The big Clark's nutcracker, as befits a denizen of the more rugged and difficult country, is reserved and wary, though not above swooping down to make off with an unguarded cracker or biscuit. When feeding on

A mountain goat leaps up a rock face, using short, powerful legs to project his 200-pound body as much as 12 feet in a single bound.

pine seeds and the like, the Clark's nutcracker performs an important natural function. With a powerful beak, the bird splits open the cones of the whitebark pines. These cones are tough, the seeds almost wingless. Without the nutcracker to throw them about and distribute some in droppings, the tree would not be able to spread its kind.

The timberline habitat also supports a few other tough seed-eaters like juncos (which seem to thrive everywhere), ravens coasting up on broad black wings for a look around, or perhaps pipits, little sparrow-like birds that live chiefly on the seeds of grasses. Once in the Tetons on a wind-blasted alpine ridge, I found a pipit's nest and clutch of eggs, even though the first autumn snowstorms were only days or weeks away. This nest was probably a second try at reproduction following the failure of a spring mating. In the late season the birds had to court, mate, build the nest, lay and incubate the eggs and rear the fledglings to the point where they could fend for themselves. The embryos in the eggs at my feet, I suspected, didn't have a chance.

You wonder that even the trees survive in this hostile environment until you look at them. On our Sawtooth trip, whenever we climbed above 8,000 feet we emerged from thick forests and entered a region of isolated and scattered trees, all uniquely adapted to the high country. Around the glacial cirques were the dark, slender symmetrical spires of subalpine firs. Their slim profiles present virtually no surface for the mountain winds to beat against; their short, downward-canted branches shed snow like a steep roof, rather than allowing it to accumulate.

Higher up on the windswept ridges were the limber pines and whitebark pines, closely related to each other—in fact virtually indistinguishable except that the limber pine has longer cones than the whitebark. Gnarled, wind-twisted to the point that their trunks were whorled like the shells of sea snails, the pines hugged the ground, their branches groping and spreading in agonized postures. Totally unlike the slender firs, they seemed not to belong up here at all, their battle apparently lost.

But when I examined them closely, I saw how they too, in a very different way, have adapted to their wind-wracked world. Their branches are so flexible as to be almost unbreakable. You can quite literally tie a branch in an overhand knot without splitting the wood. Slow-growing, resilient, these trees attain extraordinary age. John Muir once examined a stunted whitebark only three feet high and found it to be 426 years old. Not long ago near the Sawtooths, someone discovered a limber pine that proved to be 1,700 years old.

The high-country environment, so limiting to animals and birds and trees, seems to have no effect at all on the flowers, which grow in incredible profusion. One thinks of flowers flourishing only in hothouses and in the tropics. Yet some of the greatest natural floral displays belong to the forbidding world of the high mountains.

Enjoying these alpine gardens requires no botanical education, simply eyes. During the summer the hillsides are swathed in Indian paintbrush, whose tints range from deep scarlet to pale yellow. Contrasting with the paintbrushes are the deep blue bells of gentian and the rich purples of the penstemons. Other flowers carpet the moist meadows, sprout from talus slopes, and pop out of tiny pockets of soil in solid rock. You can sit high on a ridgeline so barren and exposed that you would think the hardiest lichen would have a battle for survival; but there, right in front of your nose, is a little patch of moss campion with lovely, delicate propeller-shaped blossoms. The higher you go, the smaller the plants become, yet the blossoms and leaves don't seem to diminish in size. Above timberline, Indian paintbrush may be only three inches tall; yet two inches of that will be taken up by the plant's head of bright petal-like leaves.

I have always found something uplifting in the sight of these bright displays in this most unforgiving of environments. The insouciant vitality of the flowers gives me—like the young man in folk singer John Denver's song—a kind of "Rocky Mountain High." Yet even to an amateur botanist, there is no mystery in these displays. They are simply an adaptation. Because the environment is austere, the plants here are tiny and short-stemmed, but they have big showy blossoms to compete for the attention of insects that will spread the pollen from plant to plant. All this sounds prosaic enough, but I'm afraid I am hopelessly committed to seeing in the flowers' jaunty vigor an affirmation of life's forces in the face of adversity.

Across the broad sage flats of the Stanley Basin from the Sawtooths lie the White Cloud Peaks. In the White Clouds the mountains are fewer but bigger—the monolith of Castle Peak is 11,830 feet high. Here and there among the pink granite are pale creamy eminences of sedimentary rock that make the mountains look snow-capped even when they are bone dry. The White Clouds, like the Sawtooths, are part of the Sawtooth National Recreation Area, but unlike the Sawtooths they have not been given the full protection of legal Wilderness status. They are blanketed with hundreds of mining claims, including some on the flanks

Stunted by heavy snows and twisted by gales, a dead whitebark pine squats massively on a stony Sawtooth slope.

of Castle Peak that belong to the American Smelting and Refining Company, the potential site of a huge, open-pit molybdenum mine. While most of these claims will never be worked, their existence makes conservationists nervous.

The Forest Service has other problems in the White Clouds, most of them resulting from the range's increasing attraction for trail motorcyclists, as well as foot-slogging backpackers. Hoping to learn something about these problems, I backpacked into these mountains with a young man named Paul Montague. Paul is a Forest Service wilderness ranger. He spends the summer hiking through the mountains, talking to wilderness users, reminding them about their back-country manners and cleaning up the mess left by some of the slow learners.

We drove up an old mining road from Stanley Basin, then took to the trail. We had walked only about half a mile toward Fourth of July Lake when we came to a lodgepole-pine log lying across the trail. Paul stopped and heaved it off to the side. A hundred yards farther, he had to stop again to remove another log. "What's going on?" I asked.

He laughed. "The backpackers put them here to mess up the trail-bikers," he said. There was, he explained, something of a feud between the backpackers and the people who came into the mountains on trail motorcycles. The backpackers detested the machines and were apt to boobytrap the trails with logs and rock obstacles. They even went so far as to build "whifflepoofs," logs with nails sticking out in all directions, and leave them on the trail to flatten tires.

The machines are not allowed to enter areas like the Sawtooths that have been legally designated as Wilderness, and the Forest Service has restricted them from many areas in the White Clouds. (In retaliation the bikers have sometimes ripped down the Forest Service's "Trail Closed" signs.) But on much of the public lands the bikes roam freely. In the high country their effect can be devastating. A little beyond the log barriers we came to a broad, lovely mountain meadow, so lush with blue gentian and pale yellow Indian paintbrush that I hesitated to step for fear of crushing the blossoms. But among the flowers, I saw that trail bikes had gouged foot-deep ruts, not just one but half a dozen different tracks. Looking at them, I felt a little like going back down the trail and replacing the logs.

For four days we hiked through the White Clouds. When we weren't walking I poked around like Ferdinand the Bull, looking for flowers to smell. And I tried, with little success, to entice cutthroat trout to strike at my tiny flies. Paul, meantime, trudged about picking up litter and demolishing campfire rings built of rocks. There was not very much litter, considering the amount of human use; most backpackers nowadays are very conscientious about packing out their empty tins and aluminum-foil food wrappers. But the fire rings got to Paul. "Now why," he said as he stood in front of a small Stonehenge, "when there is a fire ring right over there and another one right over there, would somebody come along and go to all the work of building this monster?"

He sighed, picked up his shovel and started tearing the ring apart, scattering the heavy rocks and covering the ashes with dirt. Indeed, some of the campsites did look as if an infantry brigade had spent the preceding night, with each squad doing its own cooking. Paul just didn't comprehend man's deep-seated instinct to improve real estate.

Throughout the White Clouds, or for that matter anywhere out here, you find evidence of this instinct, the spoor of man's urge for betterment: fire rings, lean-tos, little tables made out of logs. One campsite was neatly bordered with carefully selected rocks and looked something like a pet cemetery.

Historically, the Boy Scouts have been the worst offenders. There is something of the beaver in the Boy Scout—and it seems to come from his training. When I was a Boy Scout, in order to advance through the ranks we had to acquire something akin to a degree in civil engineering. We had to make mattresses out of fir boughs. (Put a troop of Boy Scouts to work doing this and you can ruin half a forest.) We had to make tables, benches and other furniture out of tree limbs lashed together. I tied so many lashings as a kid that I could go out in the woods tomorrow and make an Eames chair out of a pine tree and an old clothesline. At Scout camp we once spent our summer holiday spanning a little dried-up creek with a log bridge so sturdy it could have supported a locomotive.

Today, with more stress on purity in wilderness, the Boy Scouts are rapidly abandoning their Corps-of-Engineers traditions, but the urge lives on in many of us still, to the dismay of Paul and his colleagues.

These little monuments to human industry at least have the virtue of silence. One day at an alpine lake we heard the flatulent snarl of trail bikes in the distance and soon five of the little brutes appeared, lurching up out of the woods to the edge of the lake. Paul walked over to talk with the bikers and I went with him. He told them which trails were open to bikes and which were closed, and he advised them about trail conditions—where they'd find the going easy for their machines and where it would get rough. He was very polite and friendly and even-handed. The rangers make a great effort to be fair to the bikers, though most of them clearly abominate the machines. (I met one who day-dreams about hiding in ambush behind trees, sticking out his shovel to trip up the bikes one by one as they pass.)

The bikers seemed grateful for Paul's information. One middle-aged man volunteered that he'd been a backpacker himself until he had had open-heart surgery, and now the bike was the only way that he could get out into the mountains. But soon the conversation turned to car-buretors and other mechanical esoterica. After a while the open-heart man decided it was time to push on to the next lake. A gray-haired woman, apparently his wife, did not want to go just yet. She'd obvi-ously had enough of wrestling her bike up the steep trail and she was frightened of the machine. But the man prevailed and they set off. Twen-ty yards from where we were standing, at a rocky little creek, the woman fell off her bike and rolled over among the rocks. By the time we got to her, she was sitting up on the ground clutching a badly bruised knee and sobbing. The man was accusing her: "You froze up again, I told you not to freeze up."

"I know it," the woman blubbered.

"Well, why did you freeze up?"

"You told me to goose it."

"I know I told you to goose it, but you can use the brakes too."

"I know," she said, still clutching her knee and crying.

"You shouldn't have froze up."

A little later, her tears dried, they got going, the woman maneuvering her machine gingerly, as if expecting it at any moment to buck her off again. Watching them go up the trail I envied their ability to carry all their gear on their machines, which climbed the steep slope with ease. At the same time I felt a little sad for the bikers, for their machines also carried a baggage of stresses and tensions that they might well have left behind on the highway.

In a few minutes the bikes had disappeared, but for a long time their noise lingered in their wake like the sound of angry mosquitoes.

Winged Hunters

PHOTOGRAPHS BY GEORGE SILK

A great golden eagle sweeps along the rim of the Snake River Canyon, its seven-foot wings beating slowly and powerfully. Almost imperceptibly, it begins to turn, sensing an upwelling current of warm air. Again and again, the bird circles, rising higher and higher on the updraft. At last it hangs suspended at 10,000 feet, a mote in the eye of the sun.

Then, suddenly folding its wings, the eagle hurtles at more than 150 miles an hour toward the earth in the maneuver called a "stoop"—the lethal dive of a raptor, a bird of prey. From thousands of feet up, the eagle's powerful eyes have marked a squirrel in the underbrush and, talons spread, it kills.

Few spectacles in nature match the hunting flights of eagles (or their aerial courtship dances in which male and female touch talons as they pass in midflight). But to the informed observer, the fascinating and varied habits of the other raptors —the hawks, owls and falcons—are equally compelling. All are dramatically visible, perhaps as nowhere else in North America, along a 33-mile stretch of the lower Snake River in southwestern Idaho. In this preserve, established in 1971 as the Snake River Birds of Prey Natural Area, hunting of raptors is prohibited. The remoteness of the area protects the birds of prey from another major threat: the concentration of pesticides that, passed up to them through the food chain, attacks their ability to reproduce by dangerously reducing the thickness of their frail eggshells.

Roughly 20 species of raptors live in the Natural Area. The riverside cliffs provide unlimited places for nesting, and the surrounding countryside swarms with prey—jack rabbits, ground squirrels, reptiles, mice and small birds. The raptors live in natural balance with their prey, since they kill only what they need for survival. If they should overkill, there would not be enough food for all, and their own numbers would decrease as a result.

The Snake River Canyon is thus a unique place to study the raptors' powerful displays of grace and skill as the birds play out their predatory roles. On a recent trip to this area, photographer George Silk used telephoto lenses and radio-controlled cameras that had been enclosed in soundproof bags and installed within the eyries to produce the extraordinary pictorial report reproduced on the following pages.

A golden eagle surveys its domain—the canyon of the Snake River—from a narrow perch 1,000 feet above the water. The largest airborne predator in the Birds of Prey Natural Area, the golden eagle uses more hunting territory than any other raptor; there are only 53 pairs of golden eagles nesting in the 26,000-acre preserve.

A female golden eagle, powerful bill bearing a twig to build up her nest, alights at her eyrie on a canyon wall. The eaglets, only two weeks old, retain traces of their white plumage, principally on tail and wings, until they are fully mature—at five years of age.

Wary in the absence of their mother, down-covered barn owlets, only three weeks old, ignore a fresh-caught field mouse (foreground).

Owls: Silent Night Flyers

When dusk creeps up the canyon walls, the owls, having spent the daylight hours dozing in rocky crevices or hollow trees, begin to stir. Darkness is their province, and they are admirably equipped night hunters: their enormous eyes, set in their faces like human eyes to give them binocular sight, absorb a much greater amount of the available light than do the eyes of most other creatures and provide extremely acute night vision. Moreover, most owls' ears are highly sensitive: they can apparently locate and attack prey relying on sound alone. Finally, owls, called "hush-wings" by the Indians, have flight feathers that are soft as down, muffling the swish and rustle of their movement. Their prey seldom have any forewarning of danger before they feel the piercing grip of the owl's four talons.

Unlike other raptors, owls often swallow their victims whole, later regurgitating the bones and fur or feathers in compact pellets called casts. Most owls consume rats, mice and other small rodents, though some, like the seven-inch-tall pygmy owl, eat small birds and larger insects such as beetles and crickets. Owls are thus a significant factor in keeping rodent and insect populations under control.

The great horned owl, perhaps the most formidable of all the owls, kills squirrels and rabbits, and will even attack another owl that dares trespass near its nest.

A great horned owl, identifying ear tufts standing stiffly erect, glares from a rocky clifftop.

On four-foot wings, a great horned owl glides over the canyons in a rare daylight foray.

Nearly two feet tall, a red-tailed hawk, one of the larger members of the family, rests between flights in the branches of a bitterbrush.

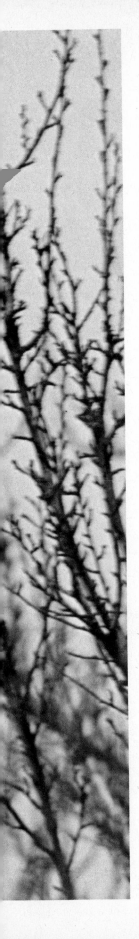

Hawks: The Sharpest Eyes in the World

At rest or aloft, the hawk is a masterful bird that conjures up an image of nobility in some ways comparable to that of the eagle. Hawks, in fact, are widely divergent: some are soarers that plummet down like eagles to pick off mammals spotted from the heights; others are low flyers that prefer to take birds—and even insects—on the wing or on the ground. Most hawks are solitary, though a few are gregarious. All are extremely sharp-eyed. The resolving power of their eyes—the ability to distinguish between distant objects—is eight times greater than man's.

Two hawks that specialize in high-altitude soaring—wheeling and gliding up to three miles above the earth —are the red-tailed and the ferruginous, or rust-colored, hawks. Some ornithologists conjecture that their flights express the hawks' exuberance and delight in their freedom.

An equally graceful soarer is Swainson's hawk, which also waits patiently on the ground for a mouse to emerge from cover. Unlike many hawks, it sometimes flies in flocks.

Dominating the air close to the tops of trees and bushes are the efficient and deadly accipiters, or bird hawks. With sudden ferocity the goshawk can surprise grouse in midflight or unwary rabbits. The goshawk's relative, the sharp-shinned hawk (named for its comparatively spindly legs) feeds on lesser birds such as sparrows, also taking its prey by stealth and ambush.

A female ferruginous hawk soars on a five-foot spread of wings, head down to scan the ground. Among the rarest species in the canyon, the ferruginous hawk is also one of the most combative—so confident of its ability to defend eggs and young that it dares build its nest on the ground.

Falcons: Swiftest of the Raptors

Falcons hold the speed record among birds of prey. Among the fastest are the peregrine falcons. A peregrine falcon's stoop has been estimated at nearly 275 miles per hour, and the bird makes as much as 60 miles per hour in level flight.

Comparatively even-tempered when trained, peregrines have been the favorites of falconers since the dawn of history. But, almost more than other raptors, they have suffered at the hands of man—not only from pesticides but also from having been trapped for their speed and potential as trained falcons. At the time of photographer Silk's visit only one member of the species had been seen in the canyon in the previous three years.

The peregrine's near-relative, the prairie falcon, ordinarily does not fly quite so fast; proportionately heavier in the body for its wings' lifting capacity than other raptors, it is nevertheless strong enough to take off without a head wind. Less threatened by man, the prairie falcon is more successful than the peregrine; about 200 members of this species live in the area.

A hunting falcon flies 50 to more than 1,000 feet above the ground. Victim spotted, the bird descends swiftly in a long, vertical or slanting dive. When the prey is another bird, the falcon will often stoop from above, knock the prey unconscious, and follow it down to the ground for a leisurely meal.

A vigilant prairie falcon, defending her nest, flies at an intruder, whose threat did not

provoke a full-scale attack; in real anger, the falcon's talons, here shown tucked under her body, would be extended for the strike.

Pulling its feet up to reduce air resistance, a prairie falcon pumps hard to take off. Though falcons' wings carry a heavier load than those of other raptors, this does not hamper them on takeoff, and their extra muscle helps them fly faster once aloft.

A prairie falcon comes in for an easy landing—talons forward, wings folding and tail down for balance and braking. The attack posture is different: in the last seconds before the end of a dive on prey, the falcon's tail stretches flat out behind and its wings may be fully spread, so that the extended talons strike the victim with the bird's full speed and weight behind them.

appear as a jagged ridge. Tallest, from left to right at center, are South Teton, Middle Teton, Grand Teton and Teewinot Mountain.

—a legendary place that swallowed up a government survey team in the 1870s—suddenly seemed all too apt. We tried to scramble down from the exposed ridge, but in the Tetons lightning storms come up with incredible speed, and we hadn't got far when hail started falling thick, with stones the size of buckshot. The hail stung, but here it was the lightning that was dangerous—well above timberline, we were the tallest things in the landscape.

We got rid of our ice axes and other metal, and the three of us crouched down low in the rocks under a single poncho while the lightning strikes moved steadily along the ridge till they were hitting the summit just above us. A strike came very close, the thunderclap simultaneous and earsplitting. We grinned at each other but not with much assurance. Hail pounded on us through the poncho. We huddled there for half an hour until the lightning moved on, and then the sun was out again, gleaming on talus slopes that were white with hail.

Peak 10,710, when we reached it, turned out not to be a real climb —just a long scrambling hike up a steep slope. We walked out onto the flat narrow summit in the late afternoon, expecting to find a little cairn or some other sign of a previous visit. But there was nothing. Looking out to our northeast we could see the soft green meadows of Alaska Basin scattered with white patches of snow and dark, near-black clumps of stunted alpine fir, and in the background the massive peaks of the main range. As far as we could tell we were the first people ever to have stood on this patch of the earth. It was not Everest but it was ours, and we wrote our names on a slip of paper and put it in a film can, built a little cairn to protect the can, and left it there so that everybody would know that we had been there first. Well, maybe not so that everybody would know; just so that we would know.

In a region where large animals can be hard to see, the south end of the Teton Range offers a rare spectacle to the winter visitor: the herds of elk that spend the cold months at the foot of Jackson Hole, and the coyotes that join the elk there. Here, at the apex of the Snake River country, lies the National Elk Refuge, a tract of some 24,000 acres of open meadow and sagebrush flats. In the winter about 8,000 elk move down to the refuge from their summer range in Yellowstone Park and the Teton Wilderness. On the refuge they feed through the winter on hay, which the refuge workers put out for them. This is a highly artificial way to deal with a herd of wild animals, but it seems unavoidable. So much of the herd's historical winter range is now occupied by man that large numbers of the animals would starve if left to forage for themselves. Even with the feeding program, about 150 elk die on the refuge during a normal winter, and thus the refuge is also the home for a large number of coyotes, who know that the winter die-off will provide easy food. In winter the refuge is, in effect, a coyote free-lunch counter.

The coyote, a small wolfish animal that weighs up to 35 pounds, has earned the enmity of some Westerners because it occasionally kills lambs. Probably no wild animal has been so harassed by man. But on the Elk Refuge all animals are protected, so it is fairly easy to observe coyotes there—a pleasant pastime since they are, God knows, far more interesting than the sheep they sometimes eat.

Predators fascinate us. Somehow the slayer is always more interesting than the slain. If a predator takes on prey of large size, as often happens, the killer must have courage and resolve: studies of mountain lions in the Idaho Primitive Area have shown that they are frequently injured by deer and other large prey, sometimes seriously. Hunting requires far more complex skills than grazing or browsing, and a keener intelligence. When you look into the eye of a coyote or one of the great cats, you get a sense of wheels turning in there, of synapses clicking, of judgments being made. Perhaps because we reasoning humans are also predators, most of us prefer dogs and cats as pets to white rabbits and hamsters; we want creatures with us that are like us.

I've always liked watching coyotes, so one day I went to the refuge with a young biologist named Franz Cominzind. Franz is one of that modern breed of biologists who study wild-animal behavior by painstakingly seeking out the creatures and observing them in their natural habitats. For several years he has, for all practical purposes, been living with coyotes. Out in the open now, Franz spotted a movement, and we focused our glasses. A large male coyote trotted through the meadow, a handsome golden-tan animal, fox red on his neck and tail. He stopped suddenly, bounded into the air and came down on his front feet. His head dropped and his tail went up like a victory flag.

"He just got a mouse," Franz said. "The reason coyotes are so successful is that they are opportunists. If there are plenty of mice they eat mice. If it's a good year for grasshoppers they'll eat grasshoppers. In a good season for rose hips they'll eat rose hips. When elk die on the refuge in winter, coyotes eat carrion. There's a saying that you could pave the entire earth, and the coyotes would still survive—they'd be living in the culverts."

Coyotes are indeed among the most adaptable creatures on earth. In efforts to exterminate them, men have employed traps, guns and unpleasant devices called getters that trigger an explosive charge to fire a cyanide capsule into the animal's mouth. For many years the federal government sponsored a massive poisoning program, using a lethal chemical called 1080, until enough conservationists objected to the practice of using public money to kill public coyotes on public lands. Yet in spite of the determined attempts to annihilate it, the coyote has not only held its own but has steadily increased its range. Once an animal of the West, it now lives anywhere from New England to Florida, and even dwells inside the city limits of Los Angeles.

The coyote's ability to survive seems clearly related to intelligence. Trying to trap live animals so that he can tag them for identification in the field, Franz Cominzind has had his hands full. One coyote undermined and then buried Cominzind's traps, apparently just for the fun of it. A female, after he'd caught her twice, learned how to steal the bait without tripping the trap.

Franz and I followed the mousing coyote for a while, trying to keep it in sight. It was aware of us but seemed unconcerned as long as we kept our distance. But the moment that we crowded it a little, approaching to within the approximate range of a rifle shot, it vanished—simply disappeared in a seemingly featureless landscape.

Farther back in the refuge we stopped to look at a den, a good-sized hole out in the sage flats. In front of it was a beaten-down patch of earth where the pups had played. Coyotes, like their big brothers the wolves, have a highly ordered society and their home lives have a certain charm. The adults are excellent providers and good parents. Coyotes do not run in packs as often as wolves do, but sometimes groups of four to six adult coyotes, perhaps blood relatives, live and hunt together. And all of the adults will feed any pups around, whether their own offspring or not. The pups are almost never left unattended, and if both parents go hunting, an aunt or bachelor uncle will stay home to babysit. The pups themselves seem to enjoy life, ambushing each other in sport and playing hide-and-seek.

Driving about with Franz and listening to him talk, I realized that he had a great respect and affection for the animals he was studying. Whatever the merits of the sheepmen's claim that coyotes damage their herds, Franz believed that indiscriminate extermination of the coyotes was wrong. But he seemed to despair of being able to get his ideas across to local people; the anticoyote prejudices ran too deep.

Late in the afternoon Franz stopped the pickup truck abruptly and

A female coyote tosses her fresh-caught prey—a live mouse—into the air. Coyotes locate mice under the snow cover by listening for their burrowing movements, then capture them with a swift pounce. Afterward the coyote will sometimes toy with its victim, rolling, tossing and pummeling it for half a minute before devouring it.

we got out. A dead coyote lay in the yellow grass. It was a young female, barely more than a pup. And she had a green tag in her ear, for
Franz had tagged her in the spring. She lay with front and back legs outstretched as if she had been running and had collapsed in the middle of
a bound. Her tongue, clamped between her teeth, curled out of her
mouth. Flies crawled in and out of her empty eye sockets. Franz knelt
over her, puzzled. Finally he turned her over and we saw that her chest
was covered with blood. He went back to the truck, got a pair of gloves
and a sharp skinning knife.

"The one part of this job I'll never get used to is cutting up animals,"
he said. Then he laid back the skin expertly, and we saw the hole in the
rib cage and the signs of hemorrhage. "Looks as if she's been shot," he
said. "Right on the refuge. Damn, it really makes me mad."

We both felt a little bit down after that, and ready to go home, but on
our way back out of the refuge Franz stopped once more, to see if he
could call up one of his animals. The coyotes' repertoire of howls and
barks, he said, was something less than a language, but seemed to be a
well-developed form of communication that conveyed information use-
ful to other coyotes. Franz thought he could recognize calls that denoted
warning, challenge, territorial occupancy, and other calls that indicate
the general emotional state of the coyote doing the howling. Now he
cupped his hands to his mouth and gave a characteristic call: two yips
followed by a long, tremulous, scalp-prickling howl. One knew instinctively what it meant: "Here I am!" Again and again he repeated the
call, and while there was something chilling about the sound, it also
seemed to me very beautiful—and very appropriate as it rang across
this open, golden land beneath the Tetons. He called again, and then
we waited, straining our ears. But no answer came.

Because of the remarkable beauty of the country, Jackson Hole and
the Tetons become a special place to people who have spent any time
there. Certainly they were for me when I was a young ranger. Fall and
early winter, in particular, were the magic times. As the summer people
emptied out, the land filled with animals. It was as if the wild creatures
had been hanging back in the wings all summer, waiting for the moment
when the valley would be theirs and they could come on stage to do
their charwoman's dance before the empty house. They came down out
of the woods, down from the mountains, down from the high Absaroka
Plateau, the redtails and the Swainson's hawks patrolling in long gentle
circles over the autumn-yellow valley, the great horned owls perching

like bulky ghosts on snow stakes, then sweeping away on ghostly wings.

The weasel, ermine now in its winter coat, coursed about the snow-covered sage flats in that tough, frantic way that a weasel has, then reared on hind legs to confront me, bobbing and weaving like a 16-ounce boxer but standing its ground and quite prepared to fight me to the death. The cow elk exploded away through the snow, and the herd bulls pranced. The Grand Teton National Park's little band of buffalo met me at the hay barn in the mornings, their placid faces hanging with icicles, and the calves sported like puppies in the new-fallen snow. On cold, clear nights when you felt the hairs freezing in your nose, the coyotes sang and yipped and ki-yied down on the lakeshore until the mountains rang with the echoes of their joy and passion.

I was 25 years old and half daffy with the beauty of it all. I saw Kit Carson in every willow thicket, and I was the first man who ever lived. I crossed Jackson Lake by canoe on a crisp-aired afternoon and saw 100 geese go over in a wedge, honking their way south. I went home to the little ranger cabin, strung a cord to hang a light bulb under the hood of my old Plymouth as a way of keeping it from freezing overnight, built a hot fire in the cabin's wood stove, and wrote the only poem I have ever written in my life. It was not a good poem, but it was a good time in a good place.

The summers were not quite so good, because of the tourists. I was not very tolerant of others' failure to share my own feelings of reverence toward the country. Once I found a man throwing rocks at a herd of elk. "Why are you doing that?" I asked.

He replied, "Because I want them to notice me."

That kind of behavior made me bitter, and it makes young rangers bitter to this day. One ranger in the Tetons recently told me he thought the park should have a chain link fence built around it, with only a handful of people allowed in at any one time. To be eligible for this privilege, one would have to pass a stiff examination to demonstrate an understanding of and appreciation for the wilderness.

I don't know whether I have grown more mellow or more cynical, but the failure of the public to respond sensitively to wilderness no longer upsets me the way it used to. I suspect that even the harried family from back East, roaring through the park at 60 miles per hour in the station wagon, is getting some benefit from the experience—even if only a sense, during the moment when they click their shutters, that there is more to the world than a pavement.

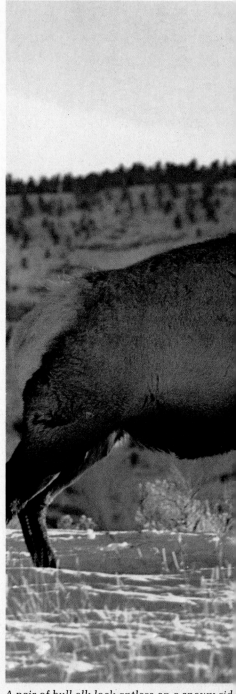

A pair of bull elk lock antlers on a snowy rid

in Wyoming. These two were probably sparring over territory; the fiercest combat, to win females, occurs in the fall mating season.

What has become more and more clear in these last few years, and especially so in the Tetons, is that the real danger comes not from those who fail to appreciate the country but from those who do. This is a national park, and thus the land is relatively secure from the kinds of attack that plague other parts of the Snake River country. There is no danger here from new dams or power plants or from logging or mining; the park is menaced not by its enemies but by its friends. Like Lennie, who lovingly crushed small, furry animals in John Steinbeck's *Of Mice and Men,* we threaten to love the place to death.

In very few places can the increase in the popularity of outdoor recreation be seen more clearly than in the Tetons. Park visitors doubled from a million and a half in the late '50s to over three million some 15 years later. In 1973 the park had almost 400,000 campers; 125,000 people hiked on the trails; almost 70,000 floated the Snake River; backpackers racked up almost 19,000 camper nights in the back country; and some 5,000 individuals signed out for climbs on the high mountains. These statistics are all the more awesome when one realizes that nearly all this use is compressed into a short summer season of 10 or 11 weeks. In 1958, if you set out to climb Grand Teton you might or might not have run into another party of two or three people on the peak. Now, during the height of the season, 50 people may climb the mountain in a day, and at critical points on the route they might have to wait in line for an hour and a half for a turn to climb.

Such heavy use produces problems and stresses that no one guessed at just a couple of decades ago. The backpackers want the horse travelers banned from the trails. The cross-country skiers, rapidly increasing in numbers, are furious at the noise and commotion caused by several thousand snowmobilers. The people who want to come in the winter to ski are in favor of an expanded airport in the valley; those who value quiet and serenity are fiercely opposed.

The heavy use has left its mark on the country itself. Trails have been gouged as much as two feet deep, high-country lakes have been polluted, and the high mountains have been left less than pristine by the sheer number of climbers. In high meadows, wild flower displays are diminished because of foot traffic—the alpine plants survive so precariously that even slight damage will prevent them from putting any of their living matter into the creation of flowers.

The response of the Park Service has been to impose a system of rules and regulations. Horses are prohibited from some trails and must carry their own feed. Some popular campsites have been closed entirely to camping to save them from permanent damage. To stop the proliferation of fire rings, all fires are now banned in the Teton back country. Camping near water is no longer permitted.

This rationing of wilderness, a heretical thought just a few years ago, is now standard practice. The very right to enter the Teton back country has been curtailed, and if one wants to make a particular trip during the height of the season he must now make a reservation in advance or wait his turn. The same is becoming true all through Snake River country. Rationing for the Sawtooth Wilderness is imminent. (Already, a camper there is not allowed to use toothpaste or soap, even biodegradable soap, for bathing or dishwashing in a lake or stream.) You have to apply months ahead of time to get a reservation to kayak or raft either the Selway River or the Middle Fork; and similar regulation is inevitable for the Salmon and Hells Canyon.

To most Americans, there is something fundamentally offensive about the proliferation of regulations governing our wilderness. Nobody ever told Daniel Boone where he could camp. Nobody ever told Jim Bridger, "Sorry, you'll have to wait till next month." Nobody ever told Kit Carson he couldn't ride over the hill to see what was on the other side for fear his horse might trample some wild flowers. Part of why we get out there is to do as we damn well please, without need to consult a committee or ask permission. Being told to go without a campfire seems a positive affront: a campfire is so much a part of camping that the two seem inseparable. If our explorers and pioneers had had to make do with a butane stove, I wonder if they would have made it past the Appalachians. On that cold October night at Holly Lake we tried to sit up and tell stories around a butane stove; forget it.

Nevertheless, most people are gradually learning to sacrifice some of their own liberties in order to save what is left of the wilderness. Hikers and backpackers accept the regulations—including the rationing system—with little complaint, and by and large they abide by the regulations. The only alternative, it appears, would be to adopt that young ranger's proposal and build a fence around the country.

Perhaps what is most surprising about the whole wild Snake River country is not how much parts of it have been trodden, trampled and transformed by armies of admirers, but how well the region has stood up to the pressure. Returning this last time, I became conscious of the resilience of the country and the creatures in it. The woodlands were still lovely, the elk herds still patrolled the open meadows, and the antelope, driven from the valley in earlier years, had moved back and were grazing out on the sagebrush flats.

I wondered how my trumpeter swans had fared. I say "my" because, in my time as a seasonal park ranger, I had felt a certain proprietary interest in a pair of these magnificent birds that used to live on a pond just over a wooded ridge behind the little ranger cabin. The trumpeters are the largest swans on the North American continent. A few decades ago they were near the brink of extinction, but in recent years, through the efforts of some determined conservationists, their numbers have increased until they form a small but healthy population in the northern Rocky Mountains.

All one summer I visited my swans several times a week as I led parties of tourists on nature walks. In the fall evenings after the tourists had gone, I strolled up over the ridge from the little cabin to check on the birds. I watched the two adults raise their four cygnets from little fuzzballs to elegantly formed, dusky gray birds almost as large as the parents themselves. But I never heard the trumpet cry for which they are named; they call only when in flight, and all summer the adults were grounded while waiting for their young to grow flight feathers.

That same year the first major snowfall came in mid-October. I walked back through the aspens, an eye out for the moose that liked to browse there, and reached the pond just at dusk. The swans were not there, and I wondered if they had flown south. As I sat there in the growing dark and the thickening snow, I heard an unearthly sound ring from the mountains—all of Purcell's brass out in the swirling snow, the horns of creation blowing in the wind. And there they came, the two huge adults, white as the snow itself, and the four gray-white cygnets, necks outstretched and wings spread like sails; still uttering their fantastic triple-tongued cry, they curved once around the pond and with a great flutter and backing of wings settled gently to the water.

It was my 26th birthday, the most beautiful moment I had ever seen in the out-of-doors, and I felt I'd got a birthday present straight from the center of creation.

A few years later a highway was rerouted to improve the approaches to a large tourist lodge. The new road ran past the swan ponds, and people speculated that the swans would leave, that they wouldn't tolerate the roar of traffic so close to their nest. And so on my last trip I went back to see what had happened, hoping perhaps to be reassured that the country and its creatures could withstand the onslaught of *us*, with our works, our burgeoning hordes and our insidious affection.

It was mid-October again, a few days shy of another birthday. I climbed over the hill through the aspens in the early evening, and it was a day much like the one I remembered. Dark and windy, gusting with snow, not soft and feathery this time but hard little pellets that stung like BBs. The leaves were gone from the wind-whipped aspens. The sere grasses and the dried leaves of balsamroot crunched under my feet. Looking back, I could see the mountains ghosting out of the clouds and the snow slanting over the willow flats. The Snake lay just to the south, and I knew how it looked on this kind of day: black, cold, with wind cat's-paws across a surface that surged like muscle.

A marsh hawk, a dove-gray male with black-tipped wings held at a dihedral, slid overhead in the wind, flying low, and disappeared beyond the near ridge. I came over the crest, and there was the pond lying below in a bowl in the sage-covered hills. The wind cut; I hunkered down in the sage and began to scan the pond with my glasses. Hundreds of ducks rode on the wind-riffled water. A raft of widgeon moved nervously away to the far side of the pond. There were four ruddies, little toy ducks with tails that stick straight up. A bufflehead: with my naked eye, I could pick out its round white head against the gray water. Pintails, mallards, gadwalls with white-flashed wings, stupid coots splattering over the water, neither running nor flying. No swans.

I could hear the occasional howl of a car passing on the highway just a couple of hundred yards behind me. I kept scanning, found a couple of redhead, then a lone ring-necked duck. Four widgeon came in fast and low, spotted me, flared away. Then, over there in the reeds on the far side, a long white neck came up like a periscope, then another. And then they came out in battle line, a great white adult in the van, three gray cygnets, then the other adult. They came stately as cruisers, gliding through water that parted before them, out into the middle of the pond. There among tiny ducks unconcerned by the regal presence that had joined them, the five trumpeters arched their necks in graceful bows, dipped their heads and began to feed.

A New-Made Land

PHOTOGRAPHS BY JAY MAISEL

The Tetons are the youngest of all the Rocky Mountains. Wrapped in morning mist or glowing in the clear sunset air, their peaks are still rising, still thrusting higher, the valleys between them deepening as the earth beneath continues to heave with the forces of creation.

The land here has a new-made look, a raw vitality and a variety of moods that are lacking in older and more worn-down regions. It is also a land of huge panoramas and vast distances cradling small pockets of secret wilderness. Photographer Jay Maisel, who took the pictures on these pages, went into Grand Teton National Park and the adjacent national forest during September, at a time when a brief autumn blends summer into winter—a time of dazzling variations of mood, of colors, of weather, of light. He emerged with the feeling that he "had seen all seasons at once. In a single vista there were fresh green plants, evergreens, brilliant fall colors and snow."

Maisel was much intrigued by the tricks played by atmospheric moisture, particularly the early-morning fogs common to Teton country in the fall. "Sometimes," he noted, "the mist closes in so tightly that it creates a pocket of wilderness only twenty feet in diameter." In so small a world the most commanding presence may be the dew-wet web of a spider. On a chilly night the moisture may take the form of hoarfrost, frozen dew, which lies gray on the grass and the ground in the long mountain shadows until midmorning, when the sun creeps along to melt it. Glittering, the particles of ice briefly reflect every color of the rainbow, turn to water and disappear. Or, perhaps, the moisture may descend as the first snow of the year.

Quaking aspen grew in many places along the trails Maisel followed. Its foliage reflected golden yellow in the water of the Snake; slender trunks, sometimes bent by the weight of past winters' snows, glowed in the long slanting light at the end of day.

Among all these irregular, varied shapes, the photographer's vision caught contrasting symmetries. At the edge of a meadow, tall alpine firs thrust out flat branches from their arrow-straight trunks in an ascending, narrowing series of cross marks. One for each year, the beautifully spaced and proportioned sets of needled branches testified to the ebullient growth of the alpine firs in that young and lovely land.

THE SOUTHWEST FACE OF GRAND TETON AT SUNSET

QUAKING ASPEN AND RED HUCKLEBERRY

WINTER-BENT ASPEN TRUNKS

HOARFROST ON A HIGH MEADOW

FIRST SNOWFALL, EARLY SEPTEMBER

SPIDER WEBS IN THE FOG

ALPINE FIR ON A GRASSY SLOPE

STUNTED SPRUCE TREES ATOP A RIDGE NEAR SHEEP CREEK CANYON

Bibliography

*Also available in paperback.
†Available only in paperback.

†Alt, David D., and Donald W. Hyndman, *Roadside Geology of the Northern Rockies*. Mountain Press Publishing Company, 1972.

Austing, G. Ronald, and John B. Holt Jr., *The World of the Great Horned Owl*. J. B. Lippincott Company, 1966.

*Bakeless, John, *Lewis and Clark: Partners in Discovery*. William Morrow and Company, 1947.

Brown, Leslie, and Dean Amadon, *Eagles, Hawks and Falcons of the World*, 2 vols. McGraw-Hill Book Company, 1968.

Cahalane, Victor H., *Mammals of North America*. Macmillan, 1947.

Coit, Margaret L., and the Editors of TIME-LIFE BOOKS, The Life History of the United States series, *The Growing Years: 1789-1829*. TIME-LIFE BOOKS, 1963.

Craighead, John J. and Frank C., Jr., and Ray J. Davis, *A Field Guide to Rocky Mountain Wildflowers*. Houghton Mifflin Company, 1963.

*DeVoto, Bernard, *The Course of Empire*. Houghton Mifflin Company, 1952.

DeVoto, Bernard, ed., *The Journals of Lewis and Clark*. Houghton Mifflin Company, 1953.

Farb, Peter, and the Editors of TIME-LIFE BOOKS, *The Land and Wildlife of North America*. TIME-LIFE BOOKS, 1966.

Federal Writers' Project, Works Progress Administration, *Idaho: A Guide in Word and Picture*. Oxford University Press, 1950.

Federal Writers' Project, Works Progress Administration, *Wyoming: A Guide to Its History, Highways and People*. Oxford University Press, 1941.

Gilbert, Bil, and the Editors of TIME-LIFE BOOKS, The Old West series, *The Trailblazers*. TIME-LIFE BOOKS, 1973.

Gulick, Bill, and photography by Earl Roberge, *Snake River Country*. The Caxton Printers, Ltd., 1971.

*Irving, Washington, *Astoria*. University of Oklahoma Press, 1964.

*Josephy, Alvin M., Jr., *The Nez Perce Indians and the Opening of the Northwest*. Yale University Press, 1971.

†Kittleman, Laurence R., *Guide to the Geology of the Owyhee Region of Oregon*. Bulletin No. 21 of the Museum of Natural History, University of Oregon, September 1973.

†Koch, Elers, *When the Mountains Roared: Stories of the 1910 Fire*. U.S. Department of Agriculture, Forest Service, no date.

†Love, J. D., and John C. Reed Jr., *Creation of the Teton Landscape*. Grand Teton Natural History Association, 1971.

Norton, Boyd, *Snake Wilderness*. Sierra Club, 1972.

Orr, Robert T., *Mammals of North America*. Doubleday & Company, Inc., 1970.

Peattie, Donald Culross, *A Natural History of Western Trees*. Bonanza Books, 1953.

*Peterson, Harold, *The Last of the Mountain Men*. Charles Scribner's Sons, 1969.

*Peterson, Roger Tory, *A Field Guide to Western Birds*. Houghton Mifflin Company, 1961.

*Scharff, Robert, ed., and the National Park Service, *Yellowstone and Grand Teton National Parks*. David McKay Company, 1966.

Seton, Ernest Thompson, *Lives of Game Animals*, vol. III, part II. Charles T. Branford, Company, 1953.

†Space, Ralph S., *The Lolo Trail*. Printcraft Printing Inc., 1970.

Spencer, Betty Goodwin, *The Big Blow-up*. The Caxton Printers, Ltd., 1956.

†Stearns, Harold T., *Geology of the Craters of the Moon National Monument, Idaho*. Craters of the Moon Natural History Association, in cooperation with the National Park Service. The Caxton Printers, Ltd., 1971.

†Urban, Karl A., *Common Plants of Craters of the Moon National Monument*. Craters of the Moon Natural History Association, Inc., in cooperation with the National Park Service, 1971.

Acknowledgments

The author and editors of this book wish to thank the following persons and institutions. In California: Suzanne H. Gallup, The Bancroft Library, University of California, Berkeley; George W. Walker, U.S. Geological Survey, Menlo Park. In Colorado: Harold E. Malde, U.S. Geological Survey, Denver; Boyd Norton, Evergreen. In Idaho: Andrew J. Arvish, Clearwater National Forest; Robert W. Reynolds, S. J. Zachwieja, Craters of the Moon National Monument, Arco; Richard Benjamin, supervisor, Challis National Forest; Ralph Pearson, Jim Simpson, Idaho Fish and Game Department, Boise; Lonn Kuck, Idaho Fish and Game Department, Salmon; Alan Defler, Emil and Penny Keck, Nezperce National Forest, Grangeville; Gary L. Harper, Sawtooth National Forest; Thomas J. Kovalicky, Paul Montague, Greg L. Munther, Gray F. Reynolds, superintendent, Sawtooth National Recreation Area, Ketchum; Robert and Carol Houghtaling, Robert McKee, St. Joe National Forest; Theodore C. Bjornn, Professor of Fishery Resources, Maurice Hornocker, Professor of Wildlife Management, Richard Naskali, Professor of Botany, University of Idaho, Moscow; Pat Benson, Ernest Day, Morlan and Pat Nelson, Boise; Jim and Anita Campbell, Cort Conley, Dean and Dee Hagmann, Jim Hendrick, Marty Huebner, Rick Petrillo, Cambridge; Floyd W. Harvey, Lewiston; Raymond J. Hoff, USDA, Forest Service, Richard Walker, Moscow; Roy Barrett, Salmon. In Montana: David F. Aldrich, Orville L. Daniels, supervisor, Bitterroot National Forest; James R. Habeck, Professor of Botany, University of Montana, Missoula; George E. Howe, Judson N. Moore, Robert W. Mutch, USDA, Forest Service, Missoula; John Meyer, Jack and Shirley Wemple, Victor. In New York City: Donald F. Bruning, Associate Curator of Ornithology, James Doherty, Associate Curator of Mammals, The New York Zoological Society; Sidney S. Horenstein, Department of Invertebrate Paleontology, The American Museum of Natural History; Martin Leifer, The New-York Historical Society; Larry G. Pardue, Plant Information Specialist, The New York Botanical Garden. In Oklahoma: Lucinda Simmons, Curator of Art, Woolaroc Museum, Bartlesville. In Oregon: Laurence R. Kittleman, Curator of Geology, Museum of Natural History, and Ewart M. Baldwin, Professor of Geology, University of Oregon, Eugene. In Pennsylvania: Mrs. Carolyn B. Milligan, American Philosophical Society Library, Philadelphia. In Washington, D.C.: George Castillo, USDA, Forest Service. In Wyoming: Joe Shellenberger, Richard Shaw, Doug McLaren, Grand Teton National Park; Jim Elder, Paul Lawrence, Jackson; Richard D. Estes, Wasatch National Forest, Mountain View.

Index

Numerals in italics indicate a photograph or drawing of the subject mentioned.